# FILM REVIEWS
## (Sex, Love and Indians)

**by Mary Scriver**

(Originally published on
www.prairiemary.blogspot.com
between MAY 14, 2006 and
AUGUST 2, 2008)

NAHPI-YAKI PRESS
PO BOX 295
VALIER, MT 59486

Copies available at www.lulu.com/prairiemary

ISBN

# IN THE CUT

This is going to be a long piece and perhaps not to the taste of some people.

I begin by reminding the reader that I came to the east slope of the Rockies in 1961 to teach English in the Blackfeet Reservation school system, which is not different from the rest of the state-supervised education districts -- in fact, was less different then than it is now. Then it was very much a white-normed school, without the Blackfeet teachers and curriculum parts that make it more specific now. I was deeper into the "dark" parts of the community than most teachers ever are, because of Bob Scriver being the City Magistrate and Justice of the Peace. I also had a lot to do with animals.

When I left here in 1973 -- reluctantly but necessarily -- I went back to Portland, OR, and became an animal control officer, what many people call a "dog catcher." I'm just beginning a book about the five years I spent doing that, but what's relevant here is that animal control is "law enforcement lite," which is to say that officers are on the same turf as regular police and -- like most emergency responders -- see a lot of extraordinary things. Out of this came an interest in "*Hill Street Blues*," the seminal cop show that mixed intense realism and considerable sex ("clean" -- as in while showering) with the weird slapstick comedy that is often part of emergencies.

I followed along with "*NYPD Blue*," which continued the same pattern, and then "*Homicide*," which was not in Manhattan anymore and lost some of the zaniness simply by being in Baltimore. It was quite a bit darker and more philosophical. I've always been a fan of the PBS English mysteries -- all costume, dialogue, and gorgeous scenery -- but thought I should check out an American series again. (I don't have regular TV or cable -- just DVD's and video.) "*The Shield*" came up among Netflix suggestions so I ordered the first season and also watched part of "*Deadwood*." "*Deadwood*" was clearly a variation on the theme of "*NYPD Blue*" with the same skinny neurotic women and the same boundary-busting villains who ironically keep order while the Gary-Cooper-earnest characters either make trouble or get killed. "*The Shield*" was again the same formula, but this time in LA where crime is a group act and the bad cops had also become a group.

The main insight that came to me about "*The Shield*" came through listening to the voice-overs of the producer/writer/director teams, who created the show as a group: the rogue cops against the corrupt system were very much a projection of maverick media guys (NO gals) who felt they were evading oppressive "suits" (money men) in order to explore real life. They had a lot of head-trippy things to say, but basically they were channeling Sipowitz without the voice-over of the sane and competent head of police. There was NO decent

Gary Cooper figure of any power -- the one dependable conscience was a middle-aged black woman. There are no model marriages.

So now I come to what I'm really writing about: a double media work called "*In the Cut*," both a book and a movie. "*In the Cut*" is slang meaning getting one's male equipment into the birth/sex canal called in slang "the Virginia" which is adorned with the "broccoli," pubic hair. It also means a place of safety. For many men, who need the comfort of women but hate their need and reject mothers or even wives, the moments of renewal are "in the cut" or "gash" or "slit." Women know this, of course, and take advantage of it even as the men take advantage of them.

The plot of "in the cut" is very simple in the book. A woman professor and collector of slang is teaching in New York City and a serial murderer -- who kills by cutting off the heads of the women -- is at large. The prof, Frannie, begins an affair with the investigating officer and is murdered. The author is a Phillipina who previously wrote "*The Lovely Bones*" which is narrated by a dead woman, a victim of violence. I haven't read it -- just about it. From her photo, she seems a lot like those thin, smart, hip female officers on "*NYPD Blues*."

In the movie, which is directed by Jane Campion, the heroine is played by Meg Ryan, who had just had failed plastic surgery before the movie was shot. (She was badly "cut.") Nicole Kidman had been scheduled to do this part and either stepped aside or had other commitments. Much is made in the online reviews about Meg Ryan trying to stay young, trying to make a career jump by taking such a hard part (highly emotional parts are always considered very difficult), but I think the change in her appearance pretty much forced her out of her previous niche and this one was a good attempt at finding a new one -- new enough that the old image wouldn't haunt her. Her face is lumpy, her hair is straight, and she appears in the nude -- evidently with a little help from a better plastic surgeon. I say all this to get it out of the way because some people stop right there.

"*In the Cut*" turned up on the "used & cheap" rack at the Valier gas station: $3. I'll watch anything for $3. (Except "*Eraserhead*" which I won't watch again for any amount of money.) Then I was in Great Falls and the book was remaindered for $5. So it was clear that I had material for a comparison. I'm an admirer of Jane Campion because I loved "*The Piano*," and I've been curious about Susanna Moore because of her earlier book, "*The Lovely Bones*." "*In the Cut*" was clearly meant to be a followup, which is at least part of the reason it ends with the death of the heroine. (Once you get a good gimmick, why let it go?) It's only 180 pages of big print, much of which is descriptions of sex. Campion took this as a framework which she covered with her own ideas, highly political and ingenious versions of the war between the sexes -- not the struggle for security in prosperity through marriage (Jane Austen), but in an equally patterned struggle for security through physical relationship. She is not so pessimistic as Edith Wharton, who felt women were hopelessly trapped in their social roles.

Campion's heroines always have a close female echo, which in this case she inflated out of a character merely mentioned in the book. The echo is Jennifer Jason Leigh, intensified from a friend to a half-sister. (There is also a "cold" echo in a sepia dream version of Meg's character's mother meeting her father while ice-skating.) No one enjoys giving decadent misery more than JJL and she really offers it up in this movie, leaving "Frannie" to seem just vague, mixed-up, and -- hey, do you suppose it's drugs? Or does she need them? The problem seems to be that she was raised in cold prosperity and never learned to form relationships. (Oh, sigh. It's so tough to be rich. Incidentally, that's JJL's background -- prosperous though hardly chilly. Her mother is a screen writer, her father an actor.)

The guys are all variations on the most blatantly phallic symbol in a while: a bright red lighthouse which is echoed in a souvenir on a desk, a drawing in the classroom, and the real thing -- which is a haven for the cops and a place of death for women. "Cornelius," the black student who defends John Wayne Gacy, is played by the same actor as one of the characters on "The Shield." He knows the slang but he don't "get" Frannie. The whole movie is a crossword puzzle of such metaphorical stuff, including the fact that Frannie teaches "*To the Lighthouse*" by VIRGINIA Wolfe. A student says "it wasn't no good because it took so long and only one woman died." "How many women have to die to make it good?" asks Frannie, sounding more like Meg Ryan than usual.

Sex, most often mixed with violence of one sort of another (the erasure of uniqueness and identity -- including plastic surgery -- is also a violence), saturates our culture. Even the most polite people constantly use symbols that point to sex. But sex is not so often seen as a symbol-system that stands for other things, perhaps parts of our culture grown even more cynical and dangerous than sex. Power, oil, war, death.

For those who can count, three women die in this movie so maybe it's a little better than the book. The third death, not in the book, is a woman found in pieces in the washing machine of the basement laundry room of her apartment building and it is the most gruesome though the "cleanest" of the deaths. But wait -- the narrator dies at the end of the book, her slate wiped clean. So that's three again.

Campion's Frannie survives because she shoots the murderer with her cop lover's (phallic symbol) gun -- which he teaches her how to use. When she practices, it is on "garbage" in a place by water ideal for dumping bodies. She has disempowered her lover by handcuffing him to a radiator pipe. Is this feminism? Or the empowerment of an individual through the disempowerment of another? (I won't pursue the homoerotic stuff, like cop partners, etc.)

For an English teacher the most interesting part is not necessarily the transit poetry that Frannie reads and records as she rides the subway, but rather her dispassionate and nonjudgmental attitude towards wickedness, even when she is the victim. This attitude seems to have had its origin in anthropology in the 19th century when Euros were constantly invading some other culture and trying to understand it but without any particular empathy.

The earliest Euro anthros on the rez were so dispassionate that they didn't really understand relationships and bowlderized the pungent mythology so it was suitable for children. Psychotherapists and psychiatrists have picked up the attitude and define everything in what is supposed to be dispassionate but -- in my opinion -- often ends up being bizaarely skewed to narcissism. (My counselor at seminary, a black Baptist minister, told me that he had doubts about me as a minister because I wasn't having sex with anyone. If I didn't have an intimate connection with one person, he said, how could I hope to be emotionally accessible to a congregation? I thought of that counselor when a weird little man came to my minsterial study to demand that I sleep with him because that's what he needed and I was there to serve his needs. What happened to theology? The relationship to God?)

So looking back at "*In the Cut*," what does it tell us once we get over the candy high of sex? I think it speaks to 1) the flight of intimacy from marriage. (The cop lover lives at home, sleeps on the sofa, but not with his wife, and only because she can't "control" the kids.) 2) The loss of connection to generativity: in the book the charm bracelet commemorates an abortion -- in the movie it's about getting married and having babies. 3) The drive to "make the cut" by "scoring," relieved only by those moments of safety "in the cut."

The corruption of the cops, the multi-ethnicity of the streets, the commodification and sentimentalization of sex (The JJL charcter lives over a topless bar where a sweet gay pimp sits by the doorway with one of his "girls" on his knee.), the weirdness of culturally supposed saviors (Kevin Bacon is a doctor who stalks Franny, carrying his Chinese Crested dog, surely the most uncuddly breed on the planet -- which Franny refuses to care for even when the Bacon character hints he will kill it.), the proliferation of tinkling Malibu Beach mobiles and Manhattan prints of tortured nudes -- it's stylized bi-coastal decadence, a presumed norm that the nation seems to agree is attractive so long as it is circumscribed. (When ministers met at our denominational headquarters in Boston, there was always one who set out to explore the red light district as a place of great fascination and supposed "reality" as in "relating to the real people." Solid farm citizens around here take their vacations at sleazy gambling cities.)

Our public distaste for political corruption and wartime death/terrorism seems to be equally matched by curiosity for "what the secret meanings are" and "exactly what happened," but no attempt is made to envision what a better world might be like or how to get to it. There is no hint that Frannie and her lover will marry and live well with happy children. We don't even know whether the characters are fertile -- evidently not and evidently immune to disease as well. The highest value is simply orgasm.

6

When people come to the reservation, they either drive through with their windows rolled up for fear of danger, or they head to the nearest bar and pick out some dangerous character to guide them through what they think will be like a movie. Unluckiest, they end up dead. Locals, especially women and children, can find protection by sticking together and creating a sort of alternative inner community which visitors rarely even imagine, which is one of the factors that makes it safe. They hide from strangers.

So this two-layered society -- Frannie and the cops' worlds versus the mysterious "normal" world of the cop's family -- is present even here on the high prairie, in a place that is supposed to be so deep into healing nature that evil can only be like the magical Brujo of *The Missing.*" It all keys into the Christian binary: above/below, saved/damned, devil/angel -- and the necessity of being extraordinarily powerful and outside the rules (god-like -- or Being President will do) in order to save the weak and innocent. (The Tommy Lee Jones character.) At least in "*The Missing*" and in the movie version of "*In the Cut*" the women (in the end) take strong action, but it seems sudden and situational.

One of the most amoral little characters I ever knew was a Blackfeet/ Philippino child raised in an urban ghetto. Lie, steal, cheat, hurt others, even destroy himself -- s/he wasn't really amoral, s/he was antimoral. Two of my male relatives -- generations back and one on each side -- were "lost" in the Philippino wars of their generation -- another U.S. interference in a troubled and different culture that left the country a shambles. (Remember that a shambles is a slaughter-house.) Both came back alcoholic and traumatized, very much like Vietnam vets. One was last seen digging a grave. Being adult is not a protection. Being male is not a protection.

But the movies insist that being in an intimate relationship with a powerful male WILL be a protection. The reservation constantly looks for an heroic man to set things right. The whole nation does the same, looking for a way to be "in the cut," "in the pink," by walling off whatever is dangerous. That wall costs money. There are other costs, which the once-fenced rez knows about, like loss of autonomy and growing dependence.

There's one other factor in this book. Mutilation by cutting, which was a practice among the Blackfeet (cutting off fingers of women and girls to show grief and cutting off noses of immoral women to punish them), and may have some relationship to Asian practices. In "The Object Stares Back: on the Nature of Seeing" by James Elkins there is a chapter called "Looking Away and Seeing Too Much." A remarkable series of photos shows a woman being executed by slicing her top to bottom with a machete. Machete deaths, even mass exterminations, have become familiar in the newspaper among people too poor to own guns. We look away and we see too much.

Of course, any feminist could tell you that cutting off women's heads keeps them from thinking, makes them manageable.

# THE WOODEN MAN'S BRIDE

"*The Wooden Man's Bride*" is a remaindered DVD, tout cheap from the Internet remainder houses such as **Hamilton** and **Daedalus**. It is one of a genre I call "Chinese Westerns," because they are about life along the Mongollian border in the 19th century where the people live in adobe houses behind big log gates and are occasionally raided by warrior renegades. Oddly, the stories are almost always about women (I read that today's Chinese women commit suicide at the rate of every four minutes.) who fight the system. The stories are often from legends. Sometimes they sound a bit like Grimm or Anderson. *Cinderella.*

In this one a bride is being carried via a chair on a servant's back and then on a dromedary (like a big woolly camel -- feet like platters) from her birth home (poor) to a marriage (wealthy). Servants have been sent to bring her -- a strong man to carry her and a resourceful woman to make sure things are done right. Servants are big in these stories, a little like the Mexicans in John Wayne SW epics.

On the way "The Whirlwind Gang" comes down on them and grabs up both the sturdy man and the bride. (They ride wonderful mustang horses like those of early Native Americans.) These events are so poignantly beautiful that any lover of dunes and long landscapes will weep. Everything is ivory (the outlaws wear unbleached cotton with angora goat vests, wool inside) except the bride who is in eye-stabbingly saturated crimson.

In the camp of the Whirlwinds, the leader (noble and cultured) sets a test of bravery for the sturdy man and he passes, so he and the bride go on to her new home. In that home the designated bridegroom has gotten all excited and intended to attack the gang, but he blundered and by accident killed himself.

His mother never blunders. In China all mothers-in-law are dowager empresses. She adheres strictly to the code. This girl has been bought, she is now the wife, and a surrogate husband is constructed of wood. He's a blockhead in the most literal sense.

Things go on from there. The sturdy man becomes the new tofu maker. Tofu is the source of the dowager's wealth and watching this 19th century technology is in itself fascinating. Again, all is cream and ivory, even the tofu.

Houses of this period and place are like Greek stages: a very patterned courtyard, platforms and walkways defined by timbers and stone, screens that open rooms into prosceniums, basic but gracefully made furniture that is carried around as needed. The huge red lanterns that were the motif of "*Raise the Red Lantern*" are here as well as the white lanterns of death. (In fact, this

8

set looks very similar -- might be the same one.) The story procedes as anyone who knows human behavior would expect.

There is an echo of foot-binding and somehow a plot point goes missing. I'm pretty sure there was a pregnancy in there somehow but it disappeared without resolution. Of course, we who watch Hollywood movies are used to this!

There is none of the kung fu high-wire leaping -- not even any sword fights -- and no bamboo grows in this part of the world. The landscape is a study in erosion and drought, which makes it eerily relevant in Montana right now, and also echoes Middle Eastern scenes. Beyond that, it is a portrayal of a time when an old rigid system is being broken up from within because it doesn't fit human lives and has lost the force it needs to impose it on them, Procrustes-style as the Greeks would say. Of course, there's always that feminist angle. But at the same time a nostalgia for a frontier, a setting in which the strong can exult and expand.

Other movies along these lines are *"Raise the Red Lantern,"* *"Farewell, my Concubine"* (much more recent in time), *"Xiu Xiu, Sent-down Girl"* (Communist revolution), and others. *"Crouching Tiger, etc."* is a very baroque example of a basically ascetic style, which may lend it some of its power.

Sometimes I kick myself for not keeping a little journal of movies seen, because I know there are more of considerable power. What the heck was the name of the one about the young wife whose husband was kicked in the family jewels by their overlord and who went in a persistent search for justice to the area committee? Again that wonderful ivory and scarlet color scheme -- with the red provided by strings of peppers drying.

Oh, this is a wonderful world to explore. I would love to see a staging of *"Antigone"* translated to early China. And personally I need the moral endorsement of stubborn women in search of justice and survival.
Two "genre" movies arrived in the mail together, purely by chance. They are so different from each other, yet similar, that I thought it would be fun to compare and contrast. One is *"Me and Mrs. Jones"* (2003) a piece of Robson Green fluff from Britain in which a Prime Minister (more like Hilary than Margaret) is romanced by a gossip columnist who is so deep in disguise that he pretends to be female and so deep in paralysis that he works for his former wife and lives in an undecorated loft with no bed.

The other is *"Revenge"* (1990) a vehicle for both Kevin Costner and the cinematographer Jeffrey Kimball, spring-boarding off Jim Harrison's novella and the success of *"Top Gun."* It was published in the same volume as and shares themes with *"Legends of the Fall"* and was supposed to have been directed by John Huston, who resisted the casting of Costner. Costner had enough clout to replace Huston with himself, which changed the balance of the film enough to offend a lot of people. The reviews are heavy with criticism of Costner. The film, which begins with extraordinary jet flying over the Mexican desert, then goes to dusty/smoky/foggy soft focus scenes of places draped with curtain sheers (sometimes rendered as tattered gauze), always with a banal TV set muttering in the background and a cage of finches twittering.

Both stories are about falling in love and the ensuing difficulties and consequences.

Harrison made enough money off his Hollywood sojourn to keep him comfortable the rest of his life, but it's clear that someone who knew movies had a firm hand here. The number and kind of characters are severely pruned, maybe moved around (The gay nurse moves from the Mennonite healer's place -- which is cut -- to the whorehouse.), and pushed towards stereotypes. The storyline works much better. Unfortunately, the texture and much of the point of the novella (forces and context of nature -- the written version begins with the barely living body of the man under a circling vulture) is lost. For instance, the elegant feathered English setter named "Doll," is replaced by a sturdy golden lab named "Rock."

Harrison was clearly doing a riff on the saying, "Revenge is a dish best served cold," so his Mennonite saver/healer is clearly into hot foods and tolerance, in contrast to the non-eating egomaniacs (though Quinn eats iced caviar with his fingers) who want revenge. The movie is a romantic pastiche meant to enhance the reputations of the actors. Anthony Quinn was to have a quadruple heart bypass just after the shooting of this movie but he is absolutely convincing. Madeleine Stowe, so graceful and porcelain, is a virginal figure of little personality. Her reverse in the movie is a rock star played by Sally Kirkland, comically corrupt. (In the print version the rock singers are movie crew and the woman is a steely actress.) The reversal of Costner is a Texas cowboy, James Gammon, who is meant to be totally repulsive, but to me he is one of the most appealing characters because he is more real. There are echoes of "*All the Pretty Horses*" or maybe the latter was the later movie, reduced in much the same way.

Both of these movies are send-ups in different ways, one that we are meant to just enjoy and one we are meant to sink into as "deep." When I checked imdb.com to see what the general public thought, it's clear that as usual they didn't. What they want is escapism (the English romance being a female escape and the Western romance being male, thus violent), but the people who liked "*Me and Mrs. Jones*" didn't bother to write reviews, I think maybe because they were mostly women. (The typical imdb.com reviewer sometimes seems to be a fourteen-year-old boy in Australia.) The men's reviews are constantly puzzled by Robson Green's appeal and Kevin Costner's LACK of whatever it is. I would identify the quality as intelligence and stage training, especially important for comedy. Even when Green is playing an emotionally blunted Asperger's victim (as in "*Wire in the Blood*") or trauma-victim (as in "*Touching Evil*"), he always shows intelligence. Costner is an overgrown kid, just reacting. Quinn has the same quality as Green. Even as a massive old man he can do a convincing take-off on himself as Zorba the Greek and make us like it.

Neither of these movies is remotely realistic. Both are spectacular: London at night, Mexico in the desert. The cultures portrayed are ritualized: always the bustling support staff for the PM and always the curandera and grubby little kids in Mexico. Try to imagine the plot of "*Revenge*" played out in England! Impossible! Try to imagine Robson Green playing the Costner part. Nope. Gotta be Harrison Ford, probably. Dunno who Huston wanted. Ford vs. Quinn would have been interesting.

With Costner, the story has got to be Oedipal -- father/son in a world based on male-bonding, which is why the "*Top Gun*" beginning works to set the tone: guys love each other in a true and pure way -- very Hemingway. Women just make trouble, even when they are most virginal and irreproachable. They still just want sex. The intellectual level is lost -- Stowe hands over one litte book and the quotes she exchanges with Costner are harmless, nothing like the body of work the two share in the story.

My one little quibble with Robson Green's story is at the end. The conceit is that he's a blocked novelist (and no wonder with an ex-wife like his, and no wonder he only slugs his replacement without vowing deathly revenge) and yet when he gets his book done it's a kid's book about a frog prince. Not much insight there. The two most clear-eyed people in this tale are the PM's daughter and Max, the female bodyguard who makes Sigourney Weaver look petite.

There's no paper equivalent for "*Me and Mrs. Jones*." It's a script, probably figured out by several people. I'm not quite sure why there needed to be a novella origin for "*Revenge*." Creds, I guess. It's interesting to consider what Huston might have done with the tale.

In the story, Cochran and Tiby are united in burying Miryea, who has been destroyed by their competitive passion for her. Cochran digs the grave, noting the striations of the soil; Tiby sits with his face in his hands. Amador, who is far more Mexican than in the movie, watches from under his sombrero. The religious (priest and nun) and the insane (the convent is an asylum) crowd close to watch.

# WHEN THE MALE LOVER DIES...

Okay, enough about romantic films in which the woman dies. How about a couple of romances where it's the man who dies? And how about if they're in Africa? Not just anyplace in Africa, but that crazy Kenya country in the Edwardian days when privileged, educated, code-observing Englishmen went to open up new country -- not with cattle ranches as in Montana, but with coffee farms. "I had a farm in Africa," says Isak Dinesen, who had to be played by Meryl Steep though the only reason for casting Robert Redford was to finance the film. He's about as British as Lily Tomlin but serves the same purpose: a little wry and astringent dialogue in a film so lush and rolling in emotion that the audience might otherwise suffocate. The trouble is that it changes the focus of his character to American-style narcissistic independence.

Both "*Out of Africa*" and "*The Flame Trees of Thika*" come out of the same Kenya coffee colonists' world. "*Flame Trees*" was copyrighted in 1959; "*Out of Africa*" in 1932. But "*Flame Trees*" as a movie was made in 1981 as a television mini-series and "*Out of Africa*" wasn't filmed until 1985. One can detect the difference in budget, though it isn't fatal. The two stories revolve around each other's success. Hayley Mills and Holly Aird are very much up to the standard of Meryl Streep.

There is a whole cluster of movies, biographies, collected letters, analyses, photos and so on, including the work of Beryl Markham, who also took a little twirl with Finch-Hatton. Maybe someday we'll have something by Peter Matthiessen out of his later experience with Kenya. It seems to have remained somehow parallel with Montana -- people have remarked that the Masai are the Blackfeet of Africa, so in a way "*Legends of the Fall*" belongs with this set of movies. (BOTH a male and a female significant other dies, one in WWI.)

The director of "*The End of the Affair*" was at pains to talk about how the affair was made possible by WWII, the disorder and the questioning of priorities and ideals. Certainly this also had to be true of the Kenya colonists, many of whom were rather adventurous veterans of what were called "country matters" in aristocratic Europe. This is quite obvious in "*Out of Africa.*" "*Flame Trees*" is necessarily more muted because of being an account through the eyes of a child. Still, Elspeth has a pretty clear idea of what goes on between Lettice (whom I have to fight to keep from calling Lettuce) and Ian.

Ben Cross is totally unlike the description of Ian, who sounds more like David Robb, the actor who plays Elspeth's father. The real Dennis Finch-Hatton was also more like David Robb, except that he was bald. Bror Blixen doesn't look particularly charismatic in photos, but Klaus Maria Brandauer always hits me dead center, because he looks like Bob Scriver. I'd have had no time for Redford if Brandauer were around. All these men are entirely different in tone and manner than the Ralph Fiennes characters who offend Whiskey Prajer.

(Maybe Fiennes suggests a Code Violator, one who lets love overrule honor.) Some people say that the most important people in the making of a film are the editor and the casting director and there's truth to that.

The civilized and honorable relationship between two men who share a woman that becomes important in *"The End of the Affair"* is also present in *"Out of Africa"* -- really rather nicely pitched exchanges between Bror and Dennis that pay off at the end when Bror has to tell Karen that her lover is dead -- and between Lettice's husband Hereward whom we dislike right off and Ian whom we are meant to love and do. But Hereward comes to grief, not because of Ian but because of his resentment of Ian. It's justified, but he's not quite strong enough to live up to the Code. A Muslim, the quintessential Code Obeyer, is the enforcer.

The women in these two movies are not at all cold, incompetent (even Lettice can play the piano) or stupid. It's mildly interesting that Kristen Scott Thomas, who was so passionately involved with Ralph Fiennes in *"The English Patient"* and so totally unlike his much warmer leading ladies in *"The End of the Affair"* and *"The Constant Gardener,"* disliked the actor Robert Redford in *"Horse Whisperer"* so much that it spoiled the movie -- her contempt showed! I'm fascinated by KST, but she is quite cool.

These love stories are like chess games. We know the moves, we know the territory. It's all strategy and style as they negotiate the context of the society, the times, even things like clothes. The equivalent of the tender little *"End of the Affair"* moment with the garter button (impossible with pantyhose) is in *"Out of Africa"* as a gentle shampoo on safari -- as compared with Bror's dry comment when Tanne wins the struggle to get supplies to him and arrives with her hair in snarls: "You've changed your hair." Somebody washed it before the tender scene in the tent, but I'm betting it wasn't Bror. Anyway, that was the night he gave her syphillis, which is very much against the code. KST is so dry she can share a bathtub with Fiennes and remain uncommitted.

One of the features the **imdb.com** database includes is a few "key words" or phrases to help bring up movies with similar themes. One keyword for *"Out of Africa"* is "self-destruction." Another is "gigolo." They seem strangely unjustified to me. Do they mean that both Karen and Dennis simply "made bad choices," as it's the fashion to say now? Dennis is hardly a gigolo. Maybe Bror is, but technically he's a husband. Is seeking adventure and mainlining adrenaline automatically "self-destruction?"

Key words for *"Flame Trees"* are "cross-cultural" and "WWI." Not cuckolded husbands. There is a major departure from the book in the video. When Tilly goes to work in the hospital (which is not described at all in the book) and Elspeth has to stay elsewhere, in the book she goes to a much wilder and higher place where she is in danger, makes friends with a "near-pygmy," but also hears the story of the Boers coming to Africa and their terrible struggle to create homesteads. It's much harder and more killing there than at the Huxley family's farm but it's mostly told as reporting rather than illustrated in scenes.

Still, this part contains much of the political and philosophical thought of the book.

In the video it's all made into an "*Anne of Green Gables*" situation with three nasty little girls and devolves into a pinafore-genre war. Tilly also has a "just girls" moment with Lettice and Mrs. Nimmo. Clearly, this was a pitch to keep families at their TV sets, at least the females, but it dilutes the honesty, the harshness, and the necessity and success of the Codes of Conduct brought by the Empire colonialists, even though it killed the men.

When I finished this post, I checked my email, working my way through the usual assortment of advertisements for converting penises into fire-hoses as a sign of male distinction. And then I looked at my photo books about Kenya in the time of these books and films. There were plenty of photos of warriors with visible penises. I doubt that any of the owners, though not English, thought of their appendages as indicators of valor. Instead, they depended upon their own Code of Conduct. No pharmaceutical can create that.

# WOMEN THROUGH THE EYES OF MEN

My two most recent Netflix movies are supposed to be based on autobiographical facts: *Tea with Mussolini* on Zefferelli's boyhood and *The End of the Affair* on Graham Greene's adulthood. Both are "unreliable," much filtered, and shaped by genre, but that little kernel of what was once fact gives them a strong anchor point which, if respected by the director and screenwriter, can give the whole story a strong spine.

For Zefferelli that kernel is the power of adult and even slightly overripe women, especially when remembered as part of the past of a little boy. His genre might be called "grande dame," a set of conventions often British and often fulfilled by English actresses. In this instance, a bit of energetic spice is added by two Yankees we're not so used to regarding this way: Cher as slightly incredible singer-star and Lily Tomlin in archeologist's drag. The script and outcome is as predictable as Commedia dell'Arte, but why complain since the interpretation is so delicious? The women are wonderful to watch and Italy is just as softly seductive as the women. The background "old women" character actors are wonderful, too, and the wicked Fascists and Germans are not very scary, even Mussolini. Some of the images are irresistible, like the defiant old ladies who have wound themselves in dynamite fuses at the end, their gauze and chiffon embellished dresses making them look like willows with vines.

*The End of the Affair*, a Greene novel that has become a bit of a chestnut even though it is well-known to be based on an actual affair he had and to whom he dedicated the book, hinges on the nature of faithfulness, both human and divine, and what kind of love can survive even death. This Irish writer and director, Loren Dutton, has successfully renewed a rather period-bound classic. Maybe it helps that he was a major Graham Greene fan in his late teenhood, which has informed him over the years. This is one time that the director's voice-over (as opposed to the plot voice-over) was VERY helpful as he went step-by-step through his decisions, explaining why he went the way he did and also frankly noting the objections and jokes of his friends while gently exposing them as shallow. The biggest change was converting the priest to a Christian believer, which is rather ironic, since Graham Greene projected his Christopher Hitchens side into what was, in his version, a "proselytizing Atheist." Dutton's point-of-view surrogate was more the naive and non-judgemental, big-eared, working class detective whose son was reassigned the port wine stain birthmark that Greene had put on the priest.

Dutton spends quite a bit of time discussing the difference between flesh in American films (vulnerable to violence) and flesh in European films (sensual and responsive). This film has the latter emphasis and Fiennes brings to it the

15

same voracious, engulfing desire he did to *The English Patient*, even miming insertion. His pubis is flashed but not hers -- just her beautiful breasts. Julianne Moore's costumes and acting are responsive, her dark hunter-green dresses with gussets behind skirt pleats that flare out orange. There was some concern about echoing *The English Patient* too much, but the decision was to ignore the concern. I don't think the echoes hurt.

Dutton also had some interesting things about rain and mirrors, their usefulness in terms of making the lighting and cinematography interesting and -- in spite of symbolic possibilities -- how they are sometimes simply light and mirrors. Ordinarily, if the story is gripping, these aspects are not obvious.

But most interesting was another change he made towards the end when a shift of both book and movie goes to the relationship between husband and lover, a kind of faithfulness based on their love of the same woman. In English fashion, they are terribly civilized and accepting of reality, with a strong sense of justice for each other. The transcendence of the woman's earthly love to the love of God is not emphasized but is there. The Fiennes character, who is defined as a novelist (and Dutton says he also is a novelist -- someone who draws on his own life and transforms it into writing) brackets the film with his typing, the sensuous act of imprinting fine paper with ink from the ribbon through the use of metal type. He turns the priest away and continues with his fierce hatred and rage. The woman has gone a place where he cannot follow.

I'm reading an interview with Stephen Toulmin, a thinker who constantly fascinates and provokes me, though I never really master what he's said. This time what struck me was his claim that somewhere a few hundred years ago we lost our belief in the real existence of a world in which we are embedded and came to the idea that all that matters is our interior construct of it, our "little person in the head" who tells us what to believe. One might say "the inner novelist" who passes judgement all the time, imposing values on what is simply there -- or seems to be. This inner self is always agitating for things to be the way it wants them and is happy enough to impose these values on other people. It's a seductive way to "be" in the world. In a movie director it's almost a necessity. But when the movie director goes home, it's best turned off. And Toulmin thinks it's time to wake from the dream and see human consciousness in all it's multi-layered, complex possibilities, while trying to understand this torrent of ambiguous bits we call the world.

Actually, I think the little person in my own head is a lot like Lily Tomlin's character in *Tea with Mussolini*. Brisk, no-nonsense, tart, loving and protective. But I do remember the fierce hunger of a needy man. And I love even the sensuosities of my little white and crystal computer keyboard.

# "AN AFFAIR OF LOVE": the Eros of Hotels

**"AN AFFAIR OF LOVE"** is a French movie, named more frankly, **"Un Liason Pornographique"** 1999.

**Roger Ebert**'s review is accurate. http://www.rogerebert.com/reviews/an-affair-of-love-2000  The trailer for the movie is not.  If you're looking for porn, the trailer is it -- hyped, naked, inaccurate, out-of-whack, cynical.  The idea of pornography is used in the title as playfully ironic.  Even when the woman in the beginning "interview" says flatly that this is a pornographic story, she is simply wrong.  Americans are too dishonest and sentimental to confront the idea of a straightforward liaison between adults, so it has to be retitled as an "affair."  It's not that either.  It is a bargain, an exploration, an experiment.  I will pursue the interview format as follows.

**How dare you watch movies like this?**

I am 75 years old, almost twice the age of this heroine who realizes that if she ever hopes to perform the sexual act she has always wanted to try, it will soon be too late.  I'm not a woman with much experience but I put no limits on what I read, so why limit film?  I'm ordained, trained to counsel for marriage, and settled with my life.  Watching publicly available DVD's quietly in my own home hardly seems like a stretch.  If not now, when?

**Where do you find them?**

Once *Netflix* adds to your algorithm anything it can code as a "type," it will send you many suggestions of what the machine considers similar.  The trouble is that they don't code for quality -- just subject.  In the end one has to resort to *Google* for help, so that's why I use the titles of books and movies as the titles of my posts.  They're meant to be found.

Actually, I was thinking about hotels and remembering meeting for a (platonic) lunch a male high income friend with a secret life who was staying in a "gentleman's hotel."  The delicacy and covertness of the staff -- I could not go up to the room, I could not dial the phone, "would madam wait over here?" -- was intriguing.  And then there was the incident when **Bob Scriver** was on *"To Tell the Truth"* and I paid for my own room in advance which turned out to be a signal that I was a prostitute.  One stumbles upon things.  So I was looking for movies about hotel liasons.

**What actually happens?**

The film begins in an utterly ordinary way: placing a classified, meeting in a cafe, negotiating payment for the hotel room at the front desk. The agenda is already agreed upon, so that's not mentioned. The woman, on entering the room, makes the familiar gesture of sitting on the edge of the bed and putting out her hand to lean on it as if testing the mattress. We do not see the undressing. In fact, we do not see what happens before they emerge, cheerful and matter-of-fact. Satisfied. Only later do we stay.

**So what DOES happen?**

Do you remember the gimmick in *"LA Law"* about "the butterfly technique" and how it was so erotically stimulating that the short nebbishy guy became a gal magnet? It was nothing but a writer's tease. There is no such thing. The closest is the elusive "g-spot."

**Then why watch?**

Because soon it becomes clear that these two people have reversed the usual pattern in American culture, which is that people fall in love and then this is the moral legitimacy and, indeed, the key to passionate sex. I've always maintained that if one is close to someone else -- I mean physically close as in sex -- cooperating and succeeding, then one begins to love the other. One does not love someone because they are beautiful, but rather when one loves someone they BECOME beautiful. It is how people who have married for convenience or politics become lovers. Remember this is the core (Cora) event in *"Downton Abbey,"* that the Earl and his American bride fall in love after years of getting to know each other. One becomes attuned.

**Does anything happen?**

An old man who uses the hotel for his trysts with prostitutes attracts their attention by having a heart attack in the hallway, involving them with his unattractive wife, his death, and the news of her suicide. Ebert sees this as reality intruding and derailing the fantasy. But I see it as deeper, a return to the idea that life is short and one ought to fulfill one's desires, but marriage can be bondage. Sex and death are so often paired.

**So they don't get married and live happily ever after?**

That's not the point. In fact, it undercuts the whole idea that this is arranged sensibly, destroys no one, simply ends. No regrets. No turning back. A second high quality movie, *"28 Hotel Rooms"* (American, 2012) explores the same premise but over a long period of time and much more explicitly. This second movie does verge on the pornographic but the relationship of the two people and their personalities, interweaving over time, was greeted with contempt by reviewers. In American terms, relationships are supposed to proceed like religious conversions. If the parties "lose faith" and simply leave, that's supposed to invalidate the process. (The American characters are married to others; the French are not.)

**Does this movie or this type of movie address the issue of discretion or even secrecy?**

Only in passing, except for the secret of what it was that the woman wanted to do with the man, which is what grabs the viewer with curiosity. Porn capitalizes on this, knowing that as children there were always tantalizing secrets among adults, esp. parents, and then -- as we realize what those secrets were -- we experience the revelations as joyful or possibly appalling. (Surely one's parents don't do THAT!!) There is always the desire for the unknown edge being rolled back, and sure enough, there is always a world of the forbidden, the exotic, the unbelievable. (*"Deep Throat"*) and then after that curiosity about who would do such things (the story of "Linda Lovelace").

This is part of the lure of sex in other cultures, religious cults, secret societies, and so on. In the interest of commodification, we ransack the lives of the poor, the displaced, the strange -- the "Other." What do they DO? What do they know that we don't? Maybe this is at the heart of torture. It can become cruel.

**Why does this issue interest you?**

In terms of the larger society, there is a fascination with what the book peddlers are now -- since the success of *"Fifty Shades of Gray "*-- calling the "dirty romance" genre. At bottom, I think these books are exploring sexual ties or at least "bonding", in hopes of decoding marriage. Any English or French person would know sex is not enough to support generations. There has to be more: economics, sharing, a larger circle of people, good work to do, some kind of home base, a theory of existence -- what's it all about in the end? Prevailing? Participation? Virtue? Desire? This is the deeper mystery.

# GETTING RID OF PEOPLE

"The House I Live In" depends quite a lot on the input of **David Simon,** the originator and writer of "*The Wire*," which is basically the same point of view in conventional fiction narrative form. A few nights ago I watched "*Why We Fight,*" by **Eugene Jarecki**, the same director who made "*The House I Live In*" and with quotes from David Simon at length. I see both movies as an attempt to move across the divide **James Flynn** described in the way people think about life. We are watching people who live in a concrete, self-circumscribed, primary experience life but watching through the mind of Simon, who is an analytical, abstract, systems thinker. In short, a Raven. If you can think with Simon, the result is galvanizing. If you cannot, go read something else. There's no use lingering around this blog.

"*The House I Live In*" is about the drug "war" in the United States, not in Columbia or Afghanistan. Nor does it blame anyone so much as it reveals a horrifying urge in all societies to get rid of those who are different, esp. if they compete with power or resources. It is not a surprise that Jarecki is Jewish and still thinking about the Nazi holocaust. Neither should you be surprised that I apply his conclusions to Irish/Scots and Blackfeet. The point is that the answers to some of our most horrifyingly tragic forces are looked at in concrete provincial terms so that we always blame individuals as rotten individuals. That way we don't have to change the social arrangements that push people into drug use.

Beyond even drugs, the causes may also account for war, famine, and AIDS. They amount to the same thing as keeping population under control by systematically killing or confining about 17% of the population, one way or another.

Here's the formula:

1. **Identification**: Who are the people we can separate from the others and that others don't particularly care about?

2. **Ostracism**: Demonize and stigmatize them so that the mainstream will pull away even farther. Never let people realize that they are human beings.

3. **Confiscation**: Begin taking their belongings as illegitimately acquired or being bad for society. This includes abstracts like the right to vote or access to subsidies. In the early days of the rez the government quietly gave land, timber and hay to the railroads without ever passing the profits on to the tribe.

4. **Concentration**: Create ghettos and gerrymander voting blocks. "Round up the usual suspects." The original reservation idea.

20

5. **Annihilation**: It's not necessary to use a machine gun. Simply make it hard for them economically, educationally, democratically, so that natural attrition -- as much an invisible hand as Adam Smith's capitalism and often the same thing -- will wear them away without anyone noticing.

So this analytic formula is brilliant, because all we have to do to reverse it is to turn it on its head. Let's use the example of Blackfeet.

1. The identification of who is Blackfeet is a major problem at present and seems like a drawback, a source of damage as people stop qualifying for tribal membership, government subsidies, employment priorities and so on. But the more it is confused -- both by the fancy definitions of provenance (misleadingly called blood quantum), by the contrasting ways of living that the people choose, by intertribal marriage, and by life off the reservation -- the harder it is to say THIS is a Blackfeet and THIS is not. Culture is even less specific and concrete. Blackfeet is becoming an abstract category. It's harder and harder to "round them up."

The hardest "identification" problem is in the concrete public mind where they remain 19th century horseback warriors.

2. Ostracizing Blackfeet gets harder all the time. There are enough now to field state representatives and to form voting blocks. Businesses cannot afford not to take their purchases and contracts seriously. Stigmatizing is easier, when the media is eager to sensationalize every sign of conflict or malfeasance, but tribal members are now lawyers and letter writers who are educated. It's easy to ostracize a staggering, slobbering individual as a concrete known person, but it's pretty hard to exclude people who look and act like everyone else. Even physically recognizing an Indian face may not be very easy these days.

3. Confiscation has been a problem since Euros confiscated the continent. Now the artifacts of the tribe are confiscated at the border when they are carried by whites or for other excuses. When there is a bottleneck where people can be held until they forfeit, there will always be temptations to use it for selfish ends. Federal and other officials are high-handed about impounding, quietly converting to private trophies, or returning to favored individuals in the tribe rather than the group as a whole. Beyond that, confiscation of land is easily managed by debts, federal and otherwise, that cannot be paid off, so result in default. The feds often seem very generous about granting money for schools or hospitals, but then might deduct the money from the profitable management of the tribal and individual assets in trust with the government.

4. Concentration on the reservation worked pretty well until wars and relocation scattered half the tribe all over the nation. Even so, there are internal concentration problems with a small community like Heart Butte or some subsidized housing plots. Stigma and ostracism within the tribe is as real

as it is between the tribe and the "outside" world. Education is the best and quickest way to scatter concentration, but it is also a form of assimilation to the larger culture. When educated tribal members return and rejoin their people, the stigma of concentration is diluted. We should be far more concerned about the concentration of Indians in prisons, but the concentration of Indians in the military appears to be a plus.

5. Annihilation was once actual, immediate, and bloody. Now it is subtle: drugs, alcohol, violence, and child neglect. Abuse of the weak, rejection of justice, and the slow erosion of cultural identity proceeds.

Much of the "help" given tribal people is in the name of "compassion," which the Blackfeet speakers often translate as "pity." The recovery of alcoholics and so on usually rejects "pity parties." The idea is to surrender to greater powers and then get to work. Easier said than done. Sovereignty taken seriously is self-reliance which CAN be protection of the entire tribe.

There is no doubt that there needs to be a curb on world overpopulation and there is no doubt that it would be easier to just pick out the 17% of the world's people that we don't like and simply machine gun them -- although it would take a while to get rid of the bodies. Some dictators have done that very directly. They weren't around to realize that the people they didn't like (intellectuals, nonconformists, artists and sexworkers) were sorely missed and damaged the quality of life for everyone. But we can watch them and learn: Pol Pot is not a good role model.

# "28 HOTEL ROOMS"

Intercourse means, besides the one you're probably already thinking, "conversation". "*28 Hotel Rooms*" is about both. "*Inter.*" Enter. "*Con.*" Connection. In a compartment called a "hotel room." A proper hotel with amenities.

This is poetry of the flesh, what bodies express.
Compartmentalized, like verses or stanzas.

There IS such a thing as bodily love -- not emotional, or reasonable, or shaped by social expectations and not lust -- just the real and deep connection to someone else's body through one's own body. Almost everyone's first love is skin-against-skin with the mother when newborns are laid all bloody and gooey on their mother's chest. Some babies develop depression symptoms after birth: the change is too severe, they are too deeply affected. The prescription is for the mother to go to bed naked with the naked (except for a diaper) baby beside her. They should stay there together for a day at least. It works. Skin-against-skin is innocent and reassuring, deeply satisfying, soul-making. In the tribal instinctive world the baby travels always against the mother in a shawl or a carry strap or a parka hood. An infant who is not embraced, stroked, kissed, will die of mirasmus. Simply giving up. The mother who does not embrace, stroke or kiss will not bond and may be grateful if the infant dies.

As adults we meet others in multiple ways, often interrupted, so that the demands of household and job, the expectations of family and partners, all interfere -- breaking off, confusing, submerging. What would it be like if two people could express skin-to-skin relationship in a compartmented place sheltered from everyday life? This is the question asked by "*28 Hotel Rooms*." Two people, matched as to age and social class; both employed in ways that let them move around the world anonymously, discretely; both emotionally mature; intelligent; self-determining but open to relationship. This is an intercourse of the bodies, without dominating or damaging. Just enough difference and change-over-time to remain interesting -- not quite enough to break the relationship.

Simple relationship is very rare. People have intense relationships via the internet that might seem protected and intimate, but they are suffused with fantasies, saturated with the skills of rhetoric, stripped of smell/taste/temperature. Everything is recorded and therefore subject to scrutiny beyond the moment, loss of secrecy, reflection that is objective and outside -- the way this movie is observed by us. Yet we are drawn in, we share as we cannot in an internet exchange.

Modern corporate life, based on global travel to conferences or speaking engagements with strangers, rarely one-on-one but rather in panels and around tables, can induce a kind of mirasmus. Separation from family, familiar environments, comfort foods. Time dislocation. Pressure of tasks. Judgment from others with power. Politics. There are plenty of films about these corrosive effects on morality and ability to relate to others. Many others about the lust for strangeness and secrecy in a luxury setting. People long for a zipless fuck, in **Erica Jong**'s phrase. But this film is neither without friction nor just a fuck.

Few know any relationships this simple and yet profound. In spite of being well-matched, the two characters are different enough to intrigue each other. She is the cool analyst; he is the extravagant poet. Yin/yang. Gender doesn't have a lot to do with it. Both are able to be present in the way of a child: curious, responding in the moment, no filtering. This is only possible to portray when actors are very skillful in a particular way that is accessible to a camera. This kind of acting originated as a "method" of establishing the reality of stage plays that portrayed relationships and society in a subtle and revealing way. It is a technique that allows the actor to inhabit the character so thoroughly and without restraint that their own inner life can show through the assumed role.

The brains of human beings, we now know and can even see with the help of electromagnetic, computer-augmented instruments, are a symphony of relationships and therefore can play many "styles" of identity, all of them valid and "true," but responsive to what is outside the person by presenting different aspects of the self. They call it the *connectome*. These two actors, **Marin Ireland** and **Chris Messina**, are so skillful that they can move in and out of the script, sometimes using memorized lines and sometimes speaking their own thoughts. In any case, their task was to create many scenes -- jazz riffs -- that could be edited into a "shaped" film by the writer/director. I haven't seen this kind of acting since auditing acting classes taught by AK. There is a kind of purity -- as opposed to intensity -- that engages empathy. This is not "bubble gum sentimentality" with a perky childish female and a prince who will make her life wonderful.

True enough, the compartmentalization and intermittence that protects this relationship, constantly renewing it, is also a confinement and interdiction that prevents some kinds of development. The naked lovers shout from their balcony at the people below: *"life is a puzzle -- help us figure it out."* That's also a description of the movie. If there were 28 hotel rooms -- chosen out of hundreds that the site managers looked at, but all in LA except for a few in NYC -- there were also hundreds of film shoots, compartmentalized and intermittent, that had to be edited as a puzzle in narrative aesthetics.

http://anthemmagazine.com/qa-with-marin-ireland/

This is a very interesting interview. Two things struck me: that Marin was in another show at the time they were shooting, so to save travel she just slept in the rooms where they shot this film: continuity.  Second, she has an intriguing theory about how to find an "eye of the storm" spot that's near the action but not in the way.  *"Nobody's talking to you and there's this bubble that you can create for yourself."*

http://www.blackbookmag.com/movies/actress-marin-ireland-talks-her-new-drama-28-hotel-rooms-1.54873  Here's another good interview that overlaps some.

http://www.aroundphilly.com/blog/2012/11/19/28-questions-for-chris-messina-about-28-hotel-rooms/  And an interview with Chris.

The different levels in considering this film include that it is a narrative in images and 28 scenes; it is a particular kind of acting; it is a genre to itself: minimum of characters, long duration shots while characters develop and think through issues; it is invented along a spine of trajectory through time. Viewers seem to wonder about conventional moral issues, not allowing any deviation from marital faithfulness. The actors involved wonder about their careers and how this film fits into them.  In real life, as friends, these two worry about protecting and supporting each other.  Probably there are ten-year-olds out there wondering whether this couple is really having sex.  The film is as pristine and self-contained as a pearl -- think about it all you like.  It remains itself.

The contrast is *"Monogamy,"* same fine cinematographer, same exuberant male actor, but all distraction, confusion, context, family, friends, kids, dog, commotion, bargaining, implications . . . the "hero" goes from photographer to voyeur to detective to stalker to -- aw, just a dawg.

# FEMALE SEX TOURISM

In reading about violence, whether between equals or imposed by a powerful person on one who is vulnerable (child, aged, female, slightly built, inebriated), the testimony that has impressed me most is the man who lost his marriage because of violence and too late realized that he had been abusive. He genuinely didn't know he was abusing his wife and children by yelling at them, insulting them and occasionally slapping or spanking them. He said every man he knew, including his birth family, acted like that. His standard was the same as for the United States in defining torture: it's okay as long as you don't damage a major organ. Bruising, cuts, and even broken bones are not considered to be damage to organs. (But skin IS an organ.) The man thought that acting this way was "keeping" order rather than destroying order. To his mind "order" was a matter of rules, HIS rules.

So now I'm going to throw a curve. Sex tourism, with female tourists. Does anyone recognize it? I recently watched *"Heading South,"* which might be considered romantic by some, soft-core porn by others and social criticism by the most sophisticated. It is based on three short stories by **Dany Laferriere**, a Haitian who now lives in Canada. The plots entangle three white women, a Wellesley professor of French literature; a conventional but needy wife from Savannah, Georgia; and a factory worker from Quebec. They are sexually taking advantage of the poverty and youth of black boys in Haiti in 1970. Living in a resort hotel where the boys are not welcome, the women swim and screw with them on the beach. The women have no sense of consequences or context, either about the boys' families or politically. Their best impulse is to take these older teens home like puppies found while on vacation, which they are sure the boys will welcome. They forget all about the American reaction to "miscegenation" or the boys' ability to manage their lives in a foreign country.

The reason I ordered the film in the first place (it streams from Netflix) is that the professor is played by **Charlotte Rampling**, whom I admire as an actress, and who is, in the plot, the character who comes the closest to understanding the situation -- not that she hesitates at all in doing what she knows is treating real human beings like something less. None of the three women is capable of recognizing their own vulnerability, their inability to distinguish between love and sex. How does a college professor have an intimate relationship between equals with an illiterate beach boy? The women all groan that they can't get laid at home, but they don't examine why that is or whether any of it is due to their own actions or whether there might be something else worth doing with their lives. The working class Quebecois woman comes closest to just staying in the moment: her lover is apparently the oldest. There is a child who aspires to being a gigolo but, to the credit of those in the story, he's rejected. In real life, he is more likely to be preferred as more easily controlled, less likely to object to anything. Neither STD's nor drugs are introduced except that the woman from Savannah is hooked on tranqs and they all drink a LOT.

The other dimension for those who are socially conscious, is that Haiti has been corrupt for a long time and runs on the rules of criminals -- "Deadwood" rules. The most appealing black lover attracts a woman "owned" by the powerful, who kill both of them and leave the naked bodies in front of the resort hotel. On the black side of the equation it is the black older male manager of the hotel who understands what's going on, but he doesn't explain very much. He is fatalistic.

This movie is actually about sex trafficking, criminal exploitation, and the American appetite for sex that fuels the system. If you think it only happens in Haiti, you're an ostrich. Think of the possibilities of a Native American reservation: poverty, lots of idle young men with considerable appeal and no particular concern for propriety, plus major romantic notions about falling madly in love with a man who wears feathers. And the inevitability of simply going back home, leaving all the difficulties behind.

The first time I saw this scenario acted out was in the early Sixties when **Ruth Beebe Hill** -- who was our guest at the time -- insisted on receiving a "wonderfully untouched young Blackfeet trapper" while she was arranged in bed. Research for her novel, *"Hanta Yo!"* maybe. The guy, who turned out to be one of our hired men, was scared to death and only stood in the doorway, so it came to nothing. We were too impressed by Hill's credentials (mostly her friendship with **Ayn Rand** which included caretaking in Rand's fancy house while pretending it was hers) but also so incredulous and amused that we did nothing to prevent this charade. Nothing happened anyway. But the pattern was there.

The point is that there is nothing simple about sex trafficking: entwined with criminals, drugs, tourism, violence, domination, privilege, and fantasy. And disease. It seems to be an impossibly coiled complex of causes. But the point of access for making change might well be simple consciousness-raising. We did it for littering, we did it for smoking, we did it for some aspects of feminism. Why can't we get people to understand that messing around with kids, even if they are boys, and esp. if there is money involved, is damaging to all concerned -- including the larger society?

The idea of wickedness has a multiple role: what the women are doing is wicked by the standards of their own society and they are titillated by it. Such swaggering boys often feel that being wicked is a source of power and even protects them. The people like the older resort manager who feels that the boys are wicked stigmatizes them. The system that supports criminals -- feeding their appetites -- is the most wicked of all. Not just the criminals -- the SYSTEM, including the fatalistic assumption that this is the natural way for things to be, so enforcing it with violence is justified. Truthfully, what else can the boys do to earn money? And the women want it.

Leferriere, I feel sure, did not write his stories for the erotic amusement of middle-class Americans who will consider this an exotic little adventure with just enough danger to be exciting. Casting an actress as strong as Rampling means that for those who are smart enough to figure it out, they will see the evil at the heart of the apple. The problem then becomes what to do about it. The solution for these women is simply to escape back to home. But there IS no escape: Haiti is entwined with America even at Wellesley. No longer can we just leave foreign countries behind, but what comes back with us is not innocent boys.

# "A CONSPIRACY OF SILENCE": 2 film reviews

There are no children in the 2003 movie about priests called *A CONSPIRACY OF SILENCE*, nor are there any Native Americans since it is about the Irish church, but it IS about the abuse of power -- which is always relevant. Actually, this would be a good vehicle for discussion to separate several problematic aspects of the priesthood.

The main focus is to argue against celibacy as a requirement for priesthood. (Some religious people try to slide the subject over to "chastity," which is slightly different.) The bases are loaded in this story: those defending celibacy are old white men who plainly have not married God, which is what they purport without realizing what mental pictures someone might form about two powerful old white men in an intimate relationship (God/Jesus as man/boy anyone?). Rather they married the Church for the power and status -- altogether a nice life -- and loyalty only to the status quo: not rocking the boat. The lesser authorities think they are enforcing immutable rules from God but the major authority thinks the rules don't really apply to him. He does what's strategic.

The kind of sexuality that must be denied in order to constitute celibacy is left open. That is, the question of whether celibacy must be the same as virginity, never ever having had any sex at all, is not addressed, except that it seems to be assumed by the community. It is clear from the plot that the only thing wrong with a "chaste" homosexual relationship (that is, faithful and nurturing) is that the church rules it wrong. The idea card about Jesus kissing John the Favorite is not played, but the church instituting the celibacy rule in the Eleventh Century is framed in terms of property, authority and greed for wealth that families might claim. NOT something Jesus prescribed. Fair enough.

No repellent gay characters exist except for the revelations about high authorities -- these days so usual in terms of secular high authorities that they've lost plot punch. Sex is framed in terms of two straight youngsters, both attractive, and an initiation so innocently seductive (a hayloft with loose hay -- not many of those now) that one *imdb.com* reviewer was horrified. The friends and family of the youngsters are in favor of this and one suggests, "Why not get out of there and go start your own parish? You'd have a crowd in the church in no time." It worked for Luther.

All same-sex lovers here are male, though there is a lesbian female who despises men and yet is sympathetic to same-sex relationships. There is just a hint at the problem of age -- an old helpless priest is the instrument of discrimination and cannot get his moral feet under him without losing his home.  One of the most important factors is the rage and helplessness of the protagonist's father, his vulnerability to the church influence on banks and government.  In the end the mask is ripped off the Archbishop so that we see that under the Church is the skull of the Mafia, quite willing to use violence.

This is not child abuse, but it is the template for child abuse, both in the home and in the church.  The same known elements of over-investment in appearance, domination, status plus a hidden vulnerability where the shriveled soul lives, craving some kind of comfort and warmth and instead passing on the suffering.  **Hugh Bonneville,** before he became responsible for "*Downton Abbey*" and the family of three girls, is here the voice of the True Christian.  (Yes, I know I'm mixing reality and fiction.)  The good guys in this movie wear colored clerical shirts with reverse collars.  They do NOT let them hang open unbuttoned the way **Jack Lennon** did.

There is a second movie by the same name, which is on YouTube.  http://www.youtube.com/watch?v=asvl6kO1Vo8  This movie IS about child abuse: a BBC documentary about a case in Nebraska in 1990.  It is a rough cut because of being cancelled mysteriously before the editing was finished.  The beginning is a Boys Town case that accuses the Catholic-sponsored beloved institution of corruption and sexual abuse of boys.  This gradually moves over to being an indictment of a small group of Nebraska big shots playing games in Washington DC and using Nebraska boys for sex and drugs.  I suspect this is one source of the constant suspicion of victim testimony, because devastating discrediting accusations were made against these kids (now adults) when they were ready to testify.  The worst tactics were deaths.  Next after that was "blaming the victim" as inherently worthless and predatory trash.  None ever recovered money settlements.  Some left in the night.

For me, a key takeaway came from one of the investigators on the side of the "righteous."  He remarked, *"This wasn't just about some old men preying on little boys, it was about really important stuff and major figures in Washington, D.C."*  Seems to me that's backwards.  The priority ought to be the little boys -- not the important big shots.  But I have no trouble at all understanding what they mean about corrupt state figures playing footsie with Washington, D.C.  That was twenty years ago.  These days the prairie state big shots fly to China and Russia.  The sex, drugs, and kids have probably not changed much.  I come from Portland, OR, where our much admired and progressive mayor was caught "shagging" the teenaged babysitter.  It was hard to believe the newspaper.

This week I've watched the first season of a new Swedish crime series called *"Annika Bentzon, Crime Reporter."*  It's fast, gorgeous, and engaging -- even with subtitles.  It appears that the idea of journalists as moralists is an idea that has not worn out, even though some of the major whistleblowers who release incriminating papers have not been treated well in Sweden.  In the BBC *"A Conspiracy of Silence,"* another source of reform comes from people of color, like the visiting alumni, a black man, who comes to give a lecture. He explicitly says in the lecture -- which is disrupted almost as soon as it is begun -- that the more farflung and supposedly "young" branches of the Roman Catholic church are far more advanced and sophisticated that the old Brit fossilized center of power, let alone Rome. So that makes four sources of renewal: media, internal people of conscience, achieving people of color, and the world-wide church.

I've also been watching TED clips all day -- those short presentations about cutting edge ideas. One of them, a man of color, says that we are being asked to assimilate as many bits of information in a day than people in medieval times had to absorb and sort in a year. This rings true. It is also one of the reasons I'm living in a small town -- not that I can evade the avalanche, but that I can reduce most of the daily stuff to near-automatic so I can think about major issues. The Internet makes research easy.

Nevertheless, there is a certain amount of paranoia that sets in. I'm not so worried about the FBI as I am that some bedraggled eight-year-old, beaten and bloody, will knock on my door late one night. Maybe he will tell me he is sexually abused. Luckily, we have a good sheriff who will confront abusers. I don't have illusions about such a boy only needing a wash-up and a new set of clothes. After the hospital, which hopefully won't discover anything that will mean a lifetime of troubles, there will need to be more than just a foster home that's sympathetic. I'm not much impressed by foster homes. And I know how twisting and distorting any abuse is to a child.

But I think it's important to try to understand what dynamics in our society make old white men with power think that their reward is permission to torture children. Why Boys Town in the first place -- created after WWI because of the many abandoned and suffering boys -- and why Jonestown? I think the questions are linked, if not overlapping. Good intentions gone not just bad but mad.

# "HIROSHIMA, MON AMOUR"

Tonight I watched for the second time the **Alain Resnais** film "*Hiroshima, Mon Amour.*" The first time was when it was released in 1960. I was a junior at Northwestern University where the Evanston movie houses were in love with foreign film. I saw it alone. It had a huge impact which I've carried embedded in me for the rest of my life, but particularly in the Sixties in Browning. I mean, I came with a high awareness of the American prairie genocide coupled with the belief that frail human abilities to love and to witness can have some impact on the future. Or even the present. It was a moral principle and it has not worn away.

If I were to make a film like this one today, it would be about a Native American and a white -- doesn't matter which gender is which. It would show an intimacy of grief against the horrific tragedy of genocide that could be as easily filmed as between two gay men facing AIDS. The cherished memories of the forbidden lover die all over again in the implacable tide of life going on. But for a brief time -- 36 hours in the case of this French actress who has fallen in love with a Japanese architect -- something forever lost is rekindled. Then lost again, but this time closer to being resolved.

One person claims to know the other person's tragedy, but that cannot be true. The Japanese man insists that the French woman does NOT know the truth about Hiroshima, though like a good liberal she has made it a point to face all the facts. Seeing photos of people cooked alive, looking at piles of hair fallen out overnight, seeing the silhouettes etched on stone walls because living people in their deaths served as stencils, is not enough. The smells, the sounds, the stunning surprise, the horrific erasure of a city, are worn away now. The ones who really knew are gone. We are left with a blizzard of origami cranes. A fancy parade. Waiting for the next bomb. Which is as likely to be dropped on us, not them. Or maybe this time the airplane will simply crash into a building.

Around here we are familiar with the white person, often a German or French person, usually female, claiming she knows all about Indians and truly understands their lives. Of course, that's ridiculous. Nevertheless, there are no less than THREE movies shooting here. I looked them up on *imdb.com*.

*"Cut Bank,"* (*Dwayne McLaren has been looking for a way out of his small town upbringing of CUT BANK, MT since he graduated high school several years earlier. When he finds himself in the wrong place at the right time, he jumps at a chance to pursue a better life in a bigger city with his girlfriend Cassandra. But luck doesn't exist in Cut Bank, and this perceived good fortune is quickly followed by a flood of bad karma.*)

*"Winter in the Blood."* (*Virgil First Raise wakes with a shiner and a hangover in a roadside ditch on the stark but beautiful plains of Montana. As he rises to face the day he sees a vision of his father lying dead at his feet. Impossible-- his father froze to death in a snowdrift years earlier. Virgil returns home to find that his wife, Agnes, has left him. Worse, she's taken his electric razor and his beloved rifle. Virgil sets out to find her-- beginning a hi-line odyssey of inebriated encounters, sexual skirmishes, and improbable cloak-and-dagger intrigues with the mysterious 'Airplane Man'. Virgil's quest also brings him face-to-face with childhood memories and visions of his beloved, lost brother Mose-- some glorious, some tragic. Only when Virgil seeks the counsel of an old, blind man named Yellow Calf, does he grasp the truth of his origins and begin to thaw the ice in his veins.*)

*"Jimmy Picard"* is a movie being made by **Benicio Del Toro** and a French director/writer/cinematographer I don't know, **Arnaud Desplechin**. It's drawn from a book that I've owned for decades and will review later: *"Reality and Dream: Psychotherapy of a Plains Indian"* by **George Devereux**. Published in 1951, it is an early attempt to understand the impact of trauma, both from hardship and abuse and from war combat. I always knew it was about a Blackfeet but thought that **"Devereaux"** (which turns out to be a "chosen" name) was Metis. Actually the author/therapist/anthropologist was French. The Indian's name is **"Everybody Talks About,"** a name I've written into a classroom grade book more than once. Quite apt this time. I don't think he's living.

*"Hiroshima, Mon Amour"* is also directed and sort of "devised" by a famous Frenchman, **Alain Renais**, who had just finished a documentary film about the German Holocaust. The script is by **Marguerite Duras**. At first *"Hiroshima"* was supposed to be a documentary about remembering the Atom Bomb drop, but we're told that gradually the center of gravity changed during development to the relationship between two tragedies: that of an obliterated city over against the woman's first love, a personal loss that pitched her into madness. In their sharing, the lovers transcend in some small part what cannot ever be diminished or forgotten. It remains an impossible tension, as unresolvable in personal life as in the public mind. And yet the forgetting begins at once.

The French and the Germans have always had a love affair with the Plains Indians. Devereaux suggests this is because their values are similar. He speaks of the "plumed Sioux." The actress who played the Frenchwoman is in her Seventies now and unrecognizable. Her movies are not known in the States. The actor who played the Japanese man is dead. He made many movies known here, like *"Woman in the Dunes"* and *"The Ugly American."* Another more recent film based on **Marguerite Duras'** writing is *"The Lover,"* which is close to autobiographical. It is a much easier film, sensual and modern. *"Hiroshima, Mon Amour"* was ground-breaking, an early sound film in black-and-white. I dislike the bombastic melodramatic sound track, but I'm not sure it would be possible to produce a remake. Too many people in international peace movements hold it in their minds as an icon. To change

the movie would be like forgetting. Anyway, mine is a minority opinion --
many admire it.

To watch this movie with the commentary is to have an excellent lesson in
movie-making, the things like cutting and framing. More than that, this is a
seamless, intense, inevitable story that remains ironically unforgettable after
all.

# "THE STONING OF SOROYA M.":
# More Than a Parable

After watching "*Lord of the Flies*" and seeing what happens when the good old Brit rules fail, it's instructive to watch "*The Stoning of Soraya M.*" and see what happens when rules are enforced, under corrupt circumstances or not. Soraya's story is true. She was a blameless wife in a small village in Iran who was accused of adultery and stoned to death. The movie was made by Iranian ex-pats who did not shrink from reality. Using a puppet, CGI, and tricky technology, the method of killing is vividly cruel. The actress playing the victim, buried in a hole to keep her from escaping, knew what was coming but when movie blood ran down her face, she was no longer acting. The full horror hit her hard. The laws in question were Sharia laws, not English Common Law, but the two movies watched together make it clear that there's more involved than just rules. So what is that?

My reference is a chapter in a **Victor Turner** book, whose ideas about liturgy I admire so much. The book is "*Dramas, Fields and Metaphors*" and the chapter is "*Passages, Margins, and Poverty: Religious Symbols of Communitas.*" He suggests that culture is always balancing structure (laws, inspectors, punishers) against *communitas* which is basic human decency and care for each other. Maybe one could say laws versus principles is the same thing; even Leviticus versus Jesus.

It's possible to go too far in either direction. Too far with law and you have Sharia stonings, too far WITHOUT law, and you have boys killing each other. But it's hard to imagine too much loving kindness unless it becomes merely indulgence with no shape or order. There are instances of communitas emerging from groups in chaos when natural leaders find expression.

Two things make the laws in "*The Stoning of Soraya M*" so horrifyingly enforceable. One is laws, rules and punishments that invade far too many realms better addressed in the modern world by counseling, separation, arbitration, and so on. (Sharia law reaches into the home, affecting sex, diet, dress and so on.)

Second, people with power use laws to punish the vulnerable, the poor, the stigmatized, the "immoral," the indigenous -- criminalizing them so the powerful can do what they like and profit from it. Too often Sharia law treats women like livestock. Lifting up of "the least of these" is urged in the stories and songs of poor people, often joined by religious persons like Jesus or St. Francis. The original Islamic movement DID include this force. Poverty becomes a solidarity and a source of kindness that is good for society as a whole. Happiness as individuals or as society depends upon successfully maintaining the tension between the two. Otherwise the result is demonstrations, revolt and guerrilla opposition.

The next series of movies that I'm watching is by **Bela Tarr**. *"Satan Tango"* is a seven hour depiction of a society so crushed by totalitarian control, poverty and corruption that life is only alcoholic misery. (It's in Hungary -- oh, poor Hungary! In the Fifties I got up to listen to the 5AM news in hopes that they'd managed to revolt! Then the US let them down, which prompted **e.e. cummings** to say, "Let's bury the Statue of Liberty because it's beginning to stink." The poets and the tricksters. also align themselves with communitas, the poor and the suffering.)

What I see around me in prairie small towns is the encouragement of "the majority rules" interpretations of democracy, instead of the communitas concept of protecting the minority. It's not quite out of control, but enough to tilt the allotment of funds towards the benefit of the rich and powerful. Cut welfare, schools, subsidies for the arts. Okay, call it Republicans versus Democrats, except that it doesn't parse out exactly.

Originally the rule of law was meant to restrain dictators, like the English kings who had the power of life and death over their subjects, like today's remnants of the Ottoman Empire. In *"The Stoning of Soraya M."* part of the dynamic was that Iran had had a dictator, the **Shah**, a tolerant leader who was open to Western-style freedoms. In the name of political freedom, the forces of **Ayatollah Khomeini** took back the country, conflating religion with secular governance. Then vengeance overran justice and once again people pretended to be God. Even in the US we intend the "rule of law" to preserve us from chaos and violence, but it must be constantly monitored and restrained to keep the government from pressing us into invasive rules. (Somebody please tell the Supreme Court.)

Reformation can finally be triggered when people are strangled by laws with disproportionate punishments. The US is going broke by incarcerating SEVEN TO TEN times more of its citizens than any other country. (Can that be true? A factoid from the radio.) Lives are destroyed. Families are broken. Commerce suffers.

In both Iran and the US the most inflammatory laws are about sex. The pill, the cost of raising children, the genome, fertility strategies, and so on have made many former rules simply obsolete. Can the 140 children of a sperm donor inherit his estate when he is already married? Bureaucratic structures like marriage are under attack from two directions. People ignore marriage by just living together, snubbing the rules as trivial and confining, with the result of confusing responsibility for finances, children, and inheritance. But on the other hand people who see marriage in the more romantic communitas sense of love and sharing want it certified for their own previously excluded kind. Such turmoil is the perfect opening for abuse. We are told that even in America today Sharia law is causing the death of women by the hands of their own family.

Our society is addressing the communitas forces through stories like this movie, even as the legislatures pass ever more complex laws, adding to the mess until we end up with something like our strangled fat tax code. The lack of realistic solutions prompts guerrilla activism: Occupy, street marches, wikileaks. Government pushbacks come in the name of law and order: the cops with pepper spray, fire hoses and truncheons. Our only hope seems to be that somehow the striving forces will produce a dialectic solution we can live with. But when?

Surely we could work out something better than trying to stone each other to death with words. The operant myth here might be the one about the hero who slew a dragon and sowed the land with its teeth. (Missile silos fill the earth around here.) They germinated and grew into ranks of soldiers. Someone threw a stone into the midst of them. The man who was struck by it turned on the next man and soon the whole company was killing each other until there was no one left. Sound like a presidential primary? Didn't Santorum just take a hit for religious conservatism?

# MOCKING "ANGEL"

"*Angel*," the 2007 movie by French director **Francois Ozon** is as much a fantasy as Harry Potter movies. It's kitch, it's camp, it's **Barbara Cartland** with a wink from **Charlotte Rampling**'s hooded eyes. A little kitten of a fantasist seems to be both telling us the story and being in it. The first half is the obligatory Cinderella tale -- the write-a-book-get-rich-and-famous-version -- so satisfactory with the clothes and the house and the big dog and, well, cats. And a devoted woman protector (sister-in-law and, well, maybe more), far more tolerant than any mother.

The second half is the tragic part, just as much a fantasy, about a scoundrel of a handsome man, who at least doesn't tell her "Frankly my dear, I don't give a damn" but, damaged by war (losing a symbolic leg), simply hangs himself from a chandelier. And she's been so ANGRY at him, but it all turns out that he loved her after all -- it was a misunderstanding and she is SO at fault! She can't see because of her silver tears. There's no sex, not really -- we're only twelve! Don't be silly! But there's SO much desire. It's just that desire fulfilled is then OVER, dahling, and then what is there to do but pet the cat. Cats.

Ozon has said that he reveals himself from behind a woman and that's what gives this the campy perfume tale about a girl, not quite a queen but certainly a princess, slipping back and forth over a knife-edge of mockery -- sometimes a little sympathy. And also a fantasy for a Frenchman of what it would be like to be an ENGLISH woman with one of those famous complexions and one of those famous houses. But not to worry -- the English publisher and his wife are pretty well anchored in reality. (If **Sam Neill** and **Charlotte Rampling** can't convey that, no one can, but it's a challenge this time around.) One has to admire the intensity -- not the truth but the candor. Actually, these two hardened cases are fond of their "Angel."

A friend has said that the LGBTX thinkers have become the most flexible and insightful on today's scene, because they have broken up their own boxed assumptions and gone to the meta-layer, the ur-culture, that the post-structuralists like so much. (If only they would be more intelligible about it!) Once a person has grasped that one's own reality is not like the realities of other lives, everything is open to question. And renewal. Which is why politicians need to be prodded out of their limos and offices. And why I like Indie movies that go somewhere totally foreign to me, though it may exist only blocks away. This was an early idea of mine. (How did I escape the box? My playmate did not. Friendship with her now is impossible.) It must have been books that freed me before 1957 when I took "Language and Thought" at Northwestern where some of my classmates were aghast to discover that other people had other worlds. Xenophobia is so American, so sit-com endorsed, so comfy.

But some of the assumptions of *"Angel"* are not just American soap. Ozon himself was consciously channeling **Lana Turner** and Scarlett O'Hara, sometimes letting the fictional dominate the actual and sometimes the other way around, but then holding back the scrim now and then to show emptiness. Dog died? Too bad -- but the new one is not so different. Mother died? Too bad. Don't let it spoil the evening. Your dress is so fabulous.

The original novelist **Elizabeth Taylor**, used the portrait as a marker. Surely Ozon knows *"La Belle Noiseuse,"* a film about a woman who insists on having her portrait painted by a gifted artist who can see her inner reality. The result is so frightening and ghastly that he walls it up so it can never been seen again. I think the original story was by **Zola**. A little of Dorian Gray in the story as well. It would be interesting for a class to discuss the juxtaposition of this movie with *"Camille Claudel"* which is taken to be an accurate depiction of a life as melodramatic and tortured as Angel's, but quite real. Claudel was Rodin's lover and a sculptor herself. Rarely does **Isabel Adjani** let her excesses quite give away that she is watching herself. (All those cats are there, cats -- the ultimate watchers.) In Ozon's movie the portrait of Angel watches over everyone's shoulders all the time, even when they're out on the front steps.

The driving ugliness that Angel's husband/painter gets her to confess and depicts in her portrait (rather successfully, I thought) is jealousy. We don't see much jealousy directly depicted until the end when she goes to see her dead husband's lover, as she deduces from a found letter, but "Angelique" is blameless, a childhood friend. Blonde, pure, innocent, and a mother. Cynical old woman that I am, I say to myself, "Yeah, sure." I wonder what the publisher's wife would think about this even more angelic Angelique..

Another rather tossed off jackstraw in this pile-up was pacifism -- Angel's hatred of war, not because she has any grasp of damage done to people (which she would deny even if she knew about it) but because it gets in her way. She's jealous of war. So many women so opposed to any violence -- surely a conversion reaction. (When you hate in the world what is actually down inside yourself.)

The main criticism in the IMDB.com notes is that people didn't know when to laugh in this movie. They understood that it was a sarcastic, mocking movie, but they couldn't see that it mixed with sympathy. They seem to think that there are certain places where there should be laughter and that perhaps, like a TV game show, a signal should be given by a laugh track or someone with a sign. But this is not laugh-out-loud material. Neither does Angel deserve stoning. It's wry recognition of ourselves. We're all a little pretentious, a little more dramatic than the facts can justify. Speaking for myself, of course. You might not be like that.

# "FAR NORTH": A Review

*"Far North"* -- sometimes called *"True North"* and easily confused with other films -- is a shamanic film. The original story was written by **Sara Maitland**. Do visit her website http://www.saramaitland.com/ She's Scots, living alone on the moor the way I live on the prairie. Well, not quite. I'm in town though it's just a village. And that's one way this story could be interpreted: the danger of being isolated, so off-the-grid that practical dangers (like an accident) are almost less important than the psychological dangers. Fear becomes a form of pride.

You'd probably better not read this review until you've watched the film. (It's on Hulu.) But if you have watched it and are trying to think about it, here are some suggestions.

A second way the story could be interpreted is in terms of the mythic matrix of the far north, the circumpolar world which is the true location of the original shamans. The woman played by **Michelle Yeoh** (marvelously) is marked by a shaman at her birth and cast out. One could argue that by the end of the story, she IS a shaman, capable of playing a "bed trick" (a deception in which a spurned lover manages to take the place of the truly chosen one, a recurring mythic theme. See **Wendy Doniger**'s noted book: *The Bedtrick: Tales of Sex and Masquerade*. It won the **Rose Mary Crawshay** prize from the British Academy for the best book about English literature written by a woman, 2002.)

A third way to approach this film is through another film: *"The Fast Runner,"* an authentic indigenous tale cast, written, directed, and shot all by indigenous people. It is also mythic, already nearly impossible to believe by people who live ordinary contemporary urban lives, but then -- in a setting mysterious and deadly -- even more powerful. That film is also about sex, but male rivals rather than female. Anyone ought to know that female rivalry is more dangerous.

The joke, the trick, in *"Far North"* is that the intruder -- that potent kiltsman **Sean Bean** -- is named Loki, the archetypal Norse trickster figure. Since tricksters and shamans are related (but not identical) the story could be interpreted as a rivalry over the girl rather than the man. If he were so clever, he ought to have found a way to "marry" both women in the common mother/daughter fantasy (one so understanding and indulgent, the other so sexually succulent).

But did you notice the cross hanging in the doorway towards the end? Maitland was a minister's wife for a long time and continues to be a devout Roman Catholic. We look for bedrock. One eternal marriage. My mother always taught me that hair meant sex! Ah, yes. It can split the rock. And combs -- combs seduce. They show up in fairy tales all the time.

There is a forecasting, foreboding, rhyme between the beginning and the end. The dog is as skillful an actor as the humans. And the blood suggested everywhere is carefully handled so we don't get grossed out. In fact, that is the smallest reindeer carcass with the fewest guts that I would have expected. Merely an indicator like many other things. It would be a mistake to get hung up on the likelihood of this and that. The beautiful hooded sheepskin jackets for instance or where that little motorboat came from and went to. I always have to restrain myself from worrying about whether the lamps will run out of oil -- cinematographers love little flames.

Another thread is the intrusion of "civilization." The soldiers with prisoners, the escapee with his crank radio, the killers of the only small social group Saiva has ever related to and the source of her baby -- all come from outside the indigenous world. When she does her final deed, the sound is the radio bringing a harsh announcer. Earlier, when first demonstrated, the radio plays the best of the outsider world: music. One could say it is the call of the "outside world" that precipitates the tragedy. Loki looks at the carving Saiva has made -- with that knife she is forever sharpening -- and says, "This is beautiful. It could be traded for something truly useful." He casts it aside.

Or another way to look at this film is as an interpretation of the human mind and the beauty of a dissociation as profound as the arctic sea, so that all emotion and motive is revealed in organic material culture: stone, skin, steel, and antler. Then it is possible that in killing the daughter who was not her own flesh and blood, and impersonating her, Saiva has been impregnated with a new beginning, a true child, just as the world plunges into the darkness of winter.

I've been writing about shamanism for the past week or so, reviewing various books. Mostly I'm writing about it to get it off the table so I can talk about liturgy and human feeling. When it comes to shamans people go in one of two naive directions. Either they see "shamanism" as a great supernatural and healing power that they can access with a few tricks or a few drugs. They do not take the danger very seriously, finding it thrilling rather than agonizing.

The other way is that they suppose "shamanism" is just a kind of religious conceit, sort of like Catholic retreat, and everyone is entitled to their little assumptions about proper ritual and values. Nothing is of REAL importance except prosperity and security. I'm pleased to have found **Ronald Grimes**' book *"Ritual Criticism"* in which he gently bumps what he calls "parashamanism," which is an oxymoron like suburban wilderness -- I mean, like, camping in the backyard where it's safe. NOT going so far north that you can be both saved and destroyed by a beautiful woman with a well-honed skinning knife.

Circumpolar shamanism, which is -- technically speaking, as **Alice Beck Kehoe** will instruct you -- really the only proper kind, is something quite specific, unaccountable and desperately final as this film depicts. A true shaman is a suffering and often twisted outcast who should be resorted to only when in extreme need. They are not your friendly neighborhood medicine man, but more like the scary brujo in *"The Missing."* The potency of their interventions is entwined with very dark powers.

# COLIN FIRTH LEADS THE WAY

Here are two **Colin Firth** movies that rhyme nicely: *"A Summer in Genoa"* (AKA *"Genova"*) and *"A Single Man."* In both movies he does us the enormous service of showing what a 21th century mensch is like. He doesn't do it alone, of course. **Michael Winterbottom** directed and **Laurence Coriat** wrote *"A Summer in Genoa."* **Tom Ford** reworked and directed **Christopher Isherwood**'s *"A Single Man."* Both Firth heroes have just been bereaved of their beloved companions, both are teachers, both are upscale, both are entirely reliable. Well, perhaps the Winterbottom character is slightly more reliable since he has two daughters. (One, Kelly, is a teenaged gazelle who in my opinion should eat more pasta but in the opinion of the local young Italian stallions is just right. The other, Mary, is in that eight/nine-year-old time of growing identity when one is vulnerable and not quite in control.) The Ford character in *"A Single Man"* drinks too much and is planning his own demise. Everyone is flirting with death. Aren't we all? All the time?

In these small intense films Firth is able to show intimacy without a sexual act. When his distraught daughter wakes in nightmare, he holds her tight, surrounding her physically but with no hint of anything salacious. With his older daughter he is physically very careful. He is aware that his older daughter is exploring sex, but manages (barely) to stay out of it. It's not that he's not attractive (female colleagues, students, friends rush to help him), it's that he accepts the full weight of responsibility. As the character in *"A Single Man,"* he enjoys the hustler and the student who approach him, but as full human beings, not just encounters. He loves his woman friend, dances with her, kisses her lightly. But that's it. In the present.

Lucky that Firth is a strong swimmer since both movies use scenes in the sea. In fact, *"A Single Man"* is haunted by his dreaming nude body twisting underwater. He manages to be competent but never exaggerated into a superman -- this is not father-as-.007. When in *Genova* he swims out to check on his nubile daughter who is sunning on a boat, it is an effort. The *Genova* film is dominated by the trope of the labyrinth because of the narrow medieval streets, so confusing and illogical, so sumptuous and sinister, so confining and yet traveled quickly if one follows them, chute-like. At one point the small crew and cast were mistaken for a family on holiday and a local woman came out to urgently warn them that the area was dangerous and they should leave immediately.

*"A Single Man"* was a little tricky to market except for the inclusion of the female character "Charlie" as a sort of beard to put on posters, but she is a full participant in the plot. With delight I recognized the sort of boy who is tenderly protective of adults. These types are new to film, I think.

*"Summer in Genoa"* never had a theatrical release, going straight to DVD. Both films are intense but demanding in terms of attention and reflection. They are made possible in part because of video filming with small steadicams tolerant of low light and able to go into very confined spaces. This in turn allows small intimate casts who bond on the set and creative crews who work together from film to film. The difference from conventional Hollywood sets and cameras is so great that it amounts to a different media, demanding both a different kind of story and a different kind of audience, much closer to the BBC repertory system that produced Colin Firth in the first place. His "breakout" role was "Mr. Darcy," a model of intelligent restraint and private affections.

So is Mr. Darcy a 21st century mensch role-model? It bears thinking about. Colin Firth, whose acting is of the sort that works by being transparent to the underlying actor, is not unlike **President Obama**, though his sympathies seem farther to the left, more like **Bono** or **Sting**. He has funded the kind of brain research that interests me, like a study of conservatives versus liberals that tried to discover differences in which of the small structures of the brain dominates each: the amygdala for the conservatives and the anterior cingulate cortex for the liberals. (I don't think that's the end of the story since some liberals are as stuck and resistant to change as any conservatives and some conservatives are open to evidence that would change their assumptions.)

When I was a kid, gazing worshipfully at **Audie Murphy** in cowboy movies, I blurred the line between the man and the actor just as everyone was meant to do. He was, after all, a war hero. But we never knew much beyond what the studio wanted us to read in publicity. The stories were predictable and patriotic. Now here's Colin Firth and we know everything and he is a world figure who speaks out about and acts out issues that are on the edge. But somehow he manages to convey the same earnest integrity that amounts to courage.

Mostly human beings guide their lives (and often their loves) by watching those around them either directly or through the media. When the media is dominated by selling and by sensational big-mouths, we are tipped in that direction. These two films about personal and domestic issues that preserve dignity and grace draw us quite different maps. Not easy ones, but coherent ones.

Though Tom Ford's film, *"A Single Man"*, is about a professor, it is also luxurious in a highly aesthetic way: an architectural gem of a house, fine cars and guns, and so on. Yet he runs to the store around the corner like an ordinary guy. His relationship with his partner is about dogs and books, relaxing together with music. Maybe the message is that part of the secret of a moral life is good taste rather than flamboyance (like Charlie's life).

Winterbottom's *"A Summer in Genoa"* is also about a professor but one who cooks and nurtures, who waits up for his teenaged daughter and respects the quite moving drawings of his younger daughter. He protects without invasion.

So maybe this message is that part of the secret of a moral life is responsible and intimate family relationships. Colin Firth is an effective messenger.

# THE RED SHOE DIARIES: Review

My red shoes.  Never worn.  My knees went out about the time I bought them and I never wore high heels after that.  These are not as high as the heels in *"The Red Shoe Diaries"* which is the name of an erotic series -- all about women who keep sad diaries about disappointed love and mail them to **David Duchovny.**  A gimmick as old as Geisha pillow books and *Penthouse.*

Of course, the original story is a **Hans Christian Anderson** fairy tale from Europe and then there's the iconic ballet movie.  But this is a little different.  Hans Anderson is always a bit dark but there's a second fairy tale that slips in here: the bit of glass from the Snow Queen's shattered mirror that prevents feeling.  Except in the Anderson tale, it's the boy who gets the glass in his eye and is frozen.  The girl, the sturdy Gerda, saves him.

In this 1992 made-for-cable-TV story the girl, **Brigitte Bako,** gets the bit of glass taken OUT of her eye and nearly instantly falls madly in love -- or lust.  She's already involved with a brainy, angry, achieving architect (Duchovny in what is said to be his "breakout" role.) but now she literally falls into the arms of a street laborer who happens to jackhammer a hole in a water pipe at that moment in a nice Freudian geyser.  He turns out to also be the salesman with the red shoes.  He's full of temptation and tricks.  (Third T is trouble.)

This is frankly erotica, but soft core.  That means the three B's: butts, backs and breasts -- as opposed to hard core porn which is the three P's: pubic, penile, penetration.  In truth, it's really more about clothes and styling.  It's one long fashion vignette except the part towards the end when the two guys take their shirts off and play basketball in the huge loft set, very **Ralph Lauren.** (**Billy Wirth**, the actor who plays the working class guy, was very impressed that the glass backboard was shattered but intact -- so classy.  He was also proud of his ball-playing "moves" but grateful that the director protected him in the, um, intimate scenes.)  The movie is full of styling touches:  a searchlight, a strong fan, champagne flutes that are two feet tall -- trombones.  A roaring fireplace.  A pinata that showers confetti, glitter, and engagement rings.  A free-standing bathtub.  All is fire and bubble bath.

The original fairy tale is about an ungrateful little girl whose kind and generous old lady benefactors keep giving her what she wants:  morocco -- or possibly patent leather -- red shoes.  (Nothing quite so fancy as what **Judy Garland** takes off the witch's feet.)  But she is never satisfied.  Then the shoes take over and begin to dance.  It's a curse.  She can't take them off.  She dances and dances and dances.  When she tries to go to church, an angel intervenes.  She goes to the executioner and gets him to use his big ax to cut off her feet (he carves her some wooden prosthetic feet) but then when she tries to go to church her feet come dancing in the red shoes and prevent her.  By now she is truly sorry.  She goes home to her tiny room and prays, penitent and devout. That angel comes back, lifts the ceiling off her room and then she's dead/transcendent -- in heaven and so pleased. Case closed.

There's no angel in this movie, though there are plenty of sexy girls. The girl -- who is rather childlike -- takes off her red shoes, gets in the tub with all her black underwear on, and slits her wrists. She has been complaining that everyone tries to control her, but no more. She wins. No heaven. (There are, however, other episodes of this series that she's in somehow.)

**Brenda Vaccaro** is a demon mother, not a nice old lady. (Absolutely fabulous green satin embroidered Chinese kimono.) This is a psychological drama -- we don't do religion these days, though there's a remarkable number of statues of angels here and there, This girl has the modern curse of more than one young contemporary woman: she has a black sucking hole in her psyche -- call it depression, call it narcissism -- and everything disappears down it. She is inconsolable. More than one man asks for advice about "high maintenance" women who cannot be filled up. Gifts, praise, vacations, sex, even mood altering pills -- and they just are never happy. They don't seem to know how. Of course, it must be all the mom's fault.

One of the most charming actors is the dog, who has become rather famous. I tried to find its name but didn't succeed. It was always there, never stole scenes, was even willing to be intimidated by this insatiable girl when she pretended to be a dog picking a fight. Some of my fav shots were someone striding across the big floor with the dog following along at just the right pace and distance, though I also liked the moment when Duchovny unlocks the gate to his apartment stairs just as a whole bag of citrus comes bouncing down at him. This is a very beautiful movie. The music, single instruments wailing the blues -- sax, muted cornet, piano -- is as lush and intense as everything else.

Wikipedia's informant says: "The soft core porn TV series, *Red Shoe Diaries* episodes were as of August 2010, running on the Canadian television channel Bravo!, early Saturday morning. From time to time, episodes can also be viewed on Showtime, on hulu.com, or for sale on DVD." Mine was Netflix, of course. Both men and women on imdb.com reported that this movie had them enthralled, but many agreed that the shorter episodes developed from this generally-praised movie were nowhere nearly as involving or skillful. Duchovny doesn't include it in his publicity.

One of the reasons I remain interested by intense but edgy films is that they do reach human patterns that are not necessarily discussed in polite company. Self-hating women who are seductive and easily seduced but then become deeply destructive are one of those patterns. I see there is a new book out about perfectionism, which is one aspect. Like many social evils, probably related to commodification of human beings. "Buy this or remain imperfect!" The glorification of manicures.

# "THE MISSING": EIGHT YEARS OLD

Last night I watched *"The Missing"* because I wanted to think about the brujo acted by **Eric Schweig**, a classic performance. But instead I found myself following the little girl. I suppose she was 8, nowhere near adolescence yet, a clear-eyed witness with very little power. I've been musing about how often this age group is the pivot point, the truth-teller, of stories. I remember my own inner life in those years as a painful time. I understood too much and yet not enough. No one paid attention to me, and maybe that's the key. At about that age the adults decide a kid is able to take care of themselves and the kids are likely to agree, seriously overestimating themselves because they have no way to really understand the danger. Eight or nine is when many kids begin to babysit younger children.

I googled, what else, and discovered eight year olds who:

1. Had been hanged by the Taliban because his father would not agree to kidnapping terms.
2. Learned to sing as a way of comforting a dying mom and now has a career as a gospel singer.
3. Were competing in beauty pageants and had botox treatments.
4. Were being tried for murder: he shot his father and another man.
5. Had been accidentally left behind on a family trip to Lourdes.
6. Was starving herself to death.
7. Was beaten by riot police in Greece
8. Decided to discontinue chemotherapy for her fatal cancer.
9. Was buried with a woman in her twenties and another younger child -- this happened about 70,000 years ago.

In short, an eight-year-old is almost like a small adult and in some cultures has been put to work in ways that make us shudder: in coal mines, as chimney sweeps, repetitious and dangerous jobs on looms and at pottery kilns. We moderns would "never" do that, right? Well, not in suburbia usually.

In *"The Wire"* there's a stunning scene in which a sixteen-year-old drug dealer is starting his day in a squat only barely inhabitable and then only because there's a long extension cord illicitly connected to a power pole. He rouses a roomful of eight-year-old kids who have slept in their clothes under thin blankets on old mattresses. He distributes to each kid a packet of snacks and a box of juice. Then he sends them off to school, checking to make sure they each have their backpacks of school books and have done their homework. To them this is normal and they accept his authority. After school they are lookouts and messengers for the drug dealers.

There's another scene in which the main police officer's two little boys, maybe 6 and 8, play spy ("front and follow") with Stringer, the most intelligent and elusive of the dealers. He never notices them, so they succeed in getting his car license number. The boys semi-understand what they're doing and why. The father, totally driven by his need to crack this case, never grasps the risk for them if they are identified by Stringer.

Long long ago my best undergrad friend gave me a copy of *"The Little Prince,"* in which **St. Exupery**, a wildly reckless and intense pilot, who has crashed in the desert, is kept company by an imaginary boy. The book is a reflection on society and friendship, a fox being the philosopher and a rose being the passionate ideal of desire. It seems that philosophy and desire are key to this age group, and yet that period in a child's development is called "latency," as though nothing were happening. I think it is when **Anthony Wallace**'s "mazeway of identity" first becomes conscious and the child begins to reflect on who he or she is, why that is, and how to become active in one's own life. Some people get stuck there.

I go searching brain studies. There's not much about eight-year-olds: "your child is growing quickly", but this is about the point in time that the physiology of arousal jumps in intensity. Kids that age can read and follow events in movies that are almost too fast for the human eye. But they are not grounded: their core is wobbly. They can't reflect or interpret. They hunger for adults who will listen. They are particularly vulnerable to predators.

In 1948, the year I turned nine, my father was in a car wreck that smashed his forehead against the windshield. Not only was he subtly changed, but the whole family reconfigured. My mother stretched to compensate. She didn't notice that I couldn't see properly and thought I read all the time because that was my personality. I was very thin, my legs ached and I had nightmares. My maternal mgrandmother died of cancer about this time. I don't remember her, but I remember her funeral. What I overheard could not be construed. And I lost access to a beloved place, the little ranch on Deer Creek. My father at this period lost tolerance and began to react violently to family disorder, even trivial kid stuff. Until then he had been a cheerful man, a family man. He was never a molester.

So at eight I was in a standard average position for a kid that age: exposed to many of the challenges of adulthood, not a baby anymore, and yet not quite able to master the situation. My moral guides were the classic fairy tales, those grim dark Euro-sermons about nasty little girls and the punishments they would earn. That must have been where I got the idea that obsessive devotion was the highest virtue, a religious idea. The notion has not served me well. People don't like being the objects of obsession. Even institutions have their doubts. Death/sex are entwined in many psychological theories, but usually from the point of view of an adult. For a child they are very much more mysterious and internal, so that they can remain unresolved for a lifetime.

Towards the end of *"The Missing,"* the stubborn little girl goes to her collapsed big sister who now understands that it's safe to fall apart. The little sister pushes the hair off the young woman's face and puts her arms around her, telling her, "Everything is all right now," soothing as though she were the mother. The viewer feels that this eight year old will not be a damaged adult. It's not so much the horror of the events, but whether there were a unified, timely, and vigorous confrontation of danger. If you can tell what it is.

# BLACK SWAN (The Movie)

The second time through *"The Black Swan"* I get it. It's a teeny-bopper fantasy that meets a grandiose narcissist abusive father fantasy ABOUT teeny-boppers. *"Growing up means sex, sex is evil and abusive, accepting it will kill you, growing up is the worst thing that can happen."* Well -- next to competing with your mother, who probably wants to be your lover if not YOU.

Wanting to be perfect is a common and destructive teeny-bopper fixation, because they are too young to know that no living thing is perfect. Perfection is paralysis which is death, so one COULD say that the drive to be perfect is what killed our little swan, our "little princess." Nabokov's version was much kinder, since Lolita simply becomes imperfect, a part of life.

Grandiose narcissist abusive fathers know nothing, NOTHING, about seduction. I mean, when the choreographer turns to the little swan's partner and demands, "Would you want to fuck this woman?" does that put her in the mood? (I thought the partner was quite sane. Even the guy in the scary wizard mask who greets the little swan backstage with a cheerful "hey"!) This story is about power-rape, sublimated through a "darker" woman who resorts to rohypnol, the date-rape drug, and makes it all the fault of the little swan that she doesn't know any better and goes mad. But tonsil-swallowing and crotch-grabbing are not turn-ons for beginners. When the dancer becomes the black swan and kisses the choreographer hard, HE doesn't respond -- just looks silly.

On the other side is the myth of the mad genius who is entitled to demand anything and dominate every woman he can. (I suppose some people are dragging Balanchine into this.) What if the little swan had met and fallen in love (remember that?) with a gentle, possibly androgenous dance partner? Quite a different story, requiring a different director. And a much different interpretation of sex.

Turning to another approach, I consult **Boria Sax**'s *"The Serpent and the Swan: The Animal Bride in Folklore and Literature."* The animal bride is a repeated figure in almost all mythology, Boria suggests possibly representing the emotional struggle with domestication, which meant separating people from wild animals in one way and bringing them closer to domestic animals in another, into a dependent relationship like a bride. "Animal bride" stories are about women (occasionally men) who are captured, usually by seizing their skins when they've temporarily taken them off. Sometimes they are bears and in coastal regions they are often seals, selkies.

Boria suggests that the earliest "animal brides" were snakes, because they take off their skins annually and can be seen doing it. Sometimes they are considered symbols of renewal, even healing. In the oldest stories they are not so much associated with Freudian penises as with Medusa's hair. But Boria believes that at some point many of the Mediterranean and European myths begin to switch from snakes to big waterbirds. He suggests the theme of "escaping" or running away might be related to migration when even pet birds will leave unless prevented some way. I will suggest that many NA tribes replenished themselves by capturing women (including whites) who might or might not bond with the new group, so that they might long to escape "home." White women who had been captured since childhood might, if "rescued", reversely long for their Indian families and homes.

This ambivalence between two worlds, expressed as human and animal, plus the shift from serpent to big bird (giving rise to feathered serpents and birds with long snaky necks) is the seed of *"Swan Lake,"* the original myth. None of this seems to have been conscious or worth consideration for **Aronovsky** who, as his alter ego states, wants a stripped-down, shockingly intense version of the tale. It sells tickets. He sees this is about schizophrenia and the extreme discipline of the body. Teeny bopper stuff. They buy tickets.

This is all background and related to what will probably be my most controversial position about this movie: sex is here portrayed as almost the same thing as Evil. Our American culture has bought into this. Violence, even lethal violence against innocent people, is okay.

"Good" ("hot") sex is always violent. It is portrayed that way. Someone on the radio yesterday joked that a US senator was called on the carpet and thrown out of office because he was a family man who loved and protected his children and had sex only with his wife in a loving private way at home in the marital bed. What an underachiever! How boring! If senators were like this, why would anyone run for office?

What a strange culture that demonizes virtue! But, of course, it demonizes and stigmatizes everything that can't be commodified. AND wickedness sells better than virtue, esp. if the wickedness means access, power, domination, pleasure. This movie is marketed as a "horror" movie, a psychological thriller, and much is made of the doppelganger, the double. Although, as the guy in the club remarks, "all you ballerinas look alike." I didn't recognize **Winona Ryder** at all. Even **Hersey** (once **"Barbara Seagull,"** remember that?) has the same bony face, big eyes, knob hairdo.

If I had the power to change one thing in this movie, I would have the CGI guys (who can do anything) create a shadowy black swan with powerful wings that would rise from the body of the white swan and soar out over the audience, though the walls of the building, and into that giant moon from the stage set.

# SOLDIER'S GIRL: Review and Reflection

Gender binaries have become so troublesome that social philosophers have begun to reflect on them. When I say "trouble," I mean murder. People are murdered because they don't fit our notions of gender binaries. I'm pondering *"Soldier's Girl,"* which is a movie version of a real event in which a soldier was bludgeoned to death as he slept -- by his fellow soldier, his dorm mate. The killer administered capital punishment for loving a person who crossed the binary division -- not just a cross dresser but a transsexual person in the process of going from male to female. Post-surgery, the relationship would no longer have been "homosexual."

This script is exemplary in its clarity, its foreshadowing of what we know will happen, and its simplicity in presenting a convincing love story. Calpurnia (**Lee Pace**) is elegant, played with dignified grace by a male actor in prosthetic breasts and a wig. She is not a campy over-the-top swish figure like the announcer at the competition she's in, but a calm, generous, balanced person whose femininity is more **Grace Kelly** than **Cher**. (Actually, she has shoulders like **Linda Evans**. I wonder whether a genital eversion amounts to as much plastic surgery as **Cher** has had. **Chas** (formerly **Chastity**) **Bono** knows for sure.)

Barry (**Troy Garity**) is a simple guy -- not too swift and not very experienced. I kept thinking about Pierre in the **Audrey Hepburn** version of *"War and Peace,"* and found out why when I went to *imdb.com* -- **Henry Fonda** played Pierre and Fonda was this actor's grandfather. Garity looks like his father, **Tom Hayden**. It's Calpurnia who is reminiscent of **Jane Fonda**, his mother.

Leggo words, assembled from particles, are unfortunate predeterminers. "Homosexual" is as misleading as "atheist." Both are stuck together from pre-existing concepts and both over-control the discussions. It is possible to be homosexual while being strongly "male" and possible to be deeply religious while not believing in God (theism).

Gender identity emerges from the interaction of a number of continuums. To which of the binary are you assigned physiologically? Even without discussing the chromosomal variations (not just xx and xy, but also xxx or xyy or broken versions with incomplete or doubled sections (sextions?) of chromosomes) and all the bodily and temperamental variations a person can be born with or develop at puberty or have traumatically imposed, common sense and ordinary experience shows that a male can be anywhere on the continuum of "maleness" in terms of size, aggression, and so on. He can be Conan the Barbarian but if his sperm isn't dynamic and fertile -- is he a male? The same for a female. She can be the most curvaceous and alluring woman of all time, but can she produce healthy babies? Which criteria are you choosing?

The aspect that crushes all the life out of discussion is desire in the sense of lust. Whom do you want to have sex with? Someone the same sex or someone of the opposite sex? But those aren't the only choices or even the controlling choices. In this movie it is clear that Barry loves elegance, high class presentation, kindness, and Calpurnia does, too, so they meet there, escaping the accusation of "low class." They are both genuine in the sense of character and they meet there in honesty and acceptance. She is knowing and he is innocent so opposites can also meet. These two are not game players.

So what about authenticity and truth? Who is putting on more of a show in drag, the singers at Visions or the soldiers in camo fatigues at the base? Is the announcer at the competition more of a cross-dresser than the female sentry at the gate in the beginning of the film?

Our culture makes a binary of gender identity more than others do. The Navajo defined many roles, some depending on what one wants to do -- the things normally done by women because they are anchored by babies or the things normally done by men who go out to hunt. In many cultures the priestly/sacred/holy people are not gender-assigned or are considered both. But they cannot be menstruating women. It's the baby part that's the big divider. But even then, an assigned nurturer is also a mother even if male.

Simpler animals sometimes have the ability to change back and forth between male and female, maybe depending on the ecology or maybe on whether there's a shortage of one or the other. Some animals carry both genders and can fertilize themselves. There is probably not a lot of pillow talk in those species (angleworms), but people do talk to themselves. (jokes) Androgeny and/or bisexuality are quiet values in some human contexts. Think **Teresias.**

No one understands how it is that an apparent man can be innerly and utterly convinced of being a woman or vice versa. It is easy to understand that some people don't fit into the culture's idea of what they ought to be and how that stigma can cause them to be targets. Ugly women, pretty men. Brainy women, ineffective men.

How did the sexual identity of "whom do you desire" get to be so important in our lives? Haven't there always been people who liked their own sex better than the opposite one? ("Liked" being a euphemism for wanting to fuck. Why so many euphemisms now that kids use the "f" word as much as combat Marines? What kind of role swap is that?) Haven't there always been people who found elements that deeply touched them and made them yearn for fusion with individuals that were not "appropriate"? (I hate that prissy word.) One of my favorite movies is *"Carrington,"* about a totally mismatched couple who were deeply in love with each other though they fucked nearly everyone in sight and the bedpost as well.

54

Why is sex the controlling moral dimension in our lives in a time when we can surgically change our bodies, chemically control our fertility, get professional help with relationships, earn money, co-habit with no license, and die for our country without regard for gender? Is that why? Is it all this freedom that makes everyone obsess so much about the subject?

Or is it that sex keeps us from thinking about violence and greed? It's not that we're all so sexually hot or why would there be such a need for Viagra? Pole-in-the-hole is not all there is to sex. REAL intercourse in the sense of physical intimacy is skin and brain: a million little physical, mental and emotional transactions of sensation that enmesh and bond and console. Otherwise, it's friction followed by a sneeze.

There are some fascinating levels to think about in this film but one of the most absorbing -- if trivial -- is the difference between fiction and reality. The real Calpurnia is certainly attractive, but in quite a different way from the movie version. The real one is almost cute, a little touch childlike. The movie version of the military camp is toned-down with a homogenized (they all look sort of cub-like) cast including tolerant hets, Asians and blacks. Testimony was that the taunts and harassment of Barry were actually much worse. **Andre Braugher** is one of my fav actors and always carries with him a kind of moral force not seen a lot in ordinary life. Barry's mother is not as I would have imagined her, but no doubt this murder was an experience that changed her.

It is my hope that this movie will help to change a culture lost in hatred and ignorance. It's not the only force for good, but it is a vivid and heart-breaking one.

# LOVE: COMPARE AND CONTRAST

My Netflix queue often clusters itself into themes, partly because I order from trailers and the trailers obey the theory that "if you liked this movie, you will also like. . ." Two films over the weekend grouped themselves around the theme "love." They could not have been more different. Not at all what I expected, partly because of their national origins and partly because of their philosophical assumptions about what love is anyway.

The first, with the shorthand title *"Amelie," for "Le Fabuleux Destin d'Amélie Poulain,"* is French. This little bagatelle is about the director's fav gamine **Audrey Tautou**, a worthy successor to **Leslie Caron** and **Audrey Hepburn**, and also about the director's home neighborhood, Montmarte, though he includes blandly "his sex shop" in the Pigalle. **Jean-Pierre Jeunet** is known in the US for directing one of the Aliens series -- a fact that could not be more misleading.

These local adventures are gathered loosely around the "parlicoot" idea, that somewhere your mate is waiting to be recognized at first sight. Strangely, Jeunet confides, there are no young male actors in France -- no **Brad Pitt** or **Leonardo diCaprio**. (Perhaps he has not noticed that they are no longer young.) So he cast a young director as the love interest. Everyone else is a character if not a caricature. But it is the set that is often the subject: blood red and pea green, it is not quite Christmas, but that kind of feverish furor of tschotskes, accumulations, iconic objects. I didn't see any salt-and-pepper shaker collections, but that doesn't mean they weren't there. Notes, signs, arrows painted on the pavement, birds significantly flying up, ringing telephones. The voice-over by Jeunet deciphers it all and makes it clear that he loved the outtakes as much as the actual movie. There are so many of them that they are on a separate disc. Tautou wears big black shoes like Minnie Mouse -- we are close to cartoon territory.

One key contribution to the amazement (maze) are his personal collection of strange stock film: a sperm penetrating an egg, a woman swelling in time-lapse pregnancy, a baby being born, babies swimming instinctively and nude, a horse that jumps the fence and joins a famous bicycle race, vaudeville acts, Pearl Bailey!! , old newsreels of war, goatherds in Afghanistan.

Another is his love of CGI and special effects, so a released goldfish (he calls it a "golden fish") turns and gazes up at the bridge from which he has been dropped into a pond. We cannot discern its emotional state. When in despair, our heroine becomes a column of water and spashes to the floor. Jeunet admits that might have been a little much. But this is a Christmas Valentine for the excessively French and sentimental, meant to cheer everyone up.

The second movie is German, "Cloud 9" or "Wolke Neun." www.metacafe.com/watch/3141122/**cloud_9_movie_**trailer/ I include a trailer (there are several) because it is guaranteed to gross-out every teenager on the planet. A married woman falls in love with a man but still loves her husband. She makes the mistake (?) of telling her husband and has to go live with the lover, which is pleasant. The husband dies. She grieves. Not remarkable except that the actors are my age! The woman is "only" 67 but the men are in their late seventies, with spindly shanks and little pot bellies. The woman is pillowy, with a nice big round bottom. They strip off their clothes (all) and make love realistically, which is to say in the groping, stuttering way that people do, not the choreographed fantasy of actors eight inches from the camera lens. Not that the camera is backed off here.

The film is garlanded with traditional German songs by a women's choir that includes the female lover. Nature, family, sweetness are offered in the words and, indeed, reviewers who loved this film called it "lyric" and bought into the sentiments -- were resentful when the plot turned dark, not considering that because the woman had a new lover, her loss of the previous one was bearable, but her choice was not without penalty.

The assumption in both films is that people fall in love at first sight. Or at least have some kind of recognizing reaction that can be developed into a whole life-changing plot turn. In the French film the key is mystery and pursuit, so that Amelie -- who loves little plots -- is forever arranging satisfying vignettes of punishment and reward. In the German film everything is explicit from the beginning. It is the simple but lyrical (it IS that) being-in-the-moment that is authentic pleasure between two people.

The review responses for *Cloud 9* are fascinating because they cover a full range. Few saw that Inge is choosing between a familiar, rather controlling, rather stiff and techie man (he will sit listening to the sounds of railroad engines) though protective (he fixes meals, takes care of her when she has flu) and a surprising, engaging, skinny-dipper who likes bicycling and long walks in nature. With the first man she has been a child and also a mother with a child, but she has not really been herself, perhaps. The review judgments depended on with which of the three characters the viewer identified -- the husband? Terrible movie, neglecting the moral issues. The lover? What a delight! Inge, the woman? "Go, Inge, go!" She seems naive, but in fact she chose the man best for a father and then the man best for a lover, painful as it was to have to choose.

What I draw from the juxtaposition of these films is that Love is a concept that depends on the context. Not only the national culture context, but also the individual characters of the persons. But whatever love is, the writer/ director's task is to depict a series of moments that evoke from the viewer something real, possibly memorable. "*Amelie*" was self-indulgent and infused with the vision of the director. "*Cloud 9*" made room for the ideas of the actors -- indeed, their realities. The color-pushed novelties and anomalies of

*"Amelie"* are fun. The gentle simplicity of ordinary essentials in *"Cloud 9"* will stay with me longer. But I'm old.

# "BIG BAD LOVE" AND SVEN BIRKERTS

Last night's movie was a terrific Indie flick, "Big Bad Love," based on a book of short stories by Larry Brown. The author takes a "rhizomatous" approach to the subject of love: love of father, mother, wife, child, best friend, place -- even when the nature of the love is negative, which mostly it is not. It is a yearning for intimacy, attachment, and sometimes devolves into obsession. But the real subject might be the mind and nature of writing as metaphor.

When I looked at the feedback at imdb.com, which is always intriguing though not always helpful except that I need the names and dates, the critics were split between loving it and hating it, vehemently so. I spent some time trying to figure this out but didn't make much headway until this morning I read Sven Birkerts' essay: http://www.theamericanscholar.org/reading-in-a-digital-age/ It has been a big hit with readers, but probably for the wrong reasons. I think most readers take it as a defense of paper books and rocks thrown at the Internet, but I don't see that. Sven frames the problem as the difference between the novel, which I'm going to put into quotes, since I think the "novel" has come to represent any writing that offers a personal sensibility as opposed to "objective reasoning." I put THAT in quotes because I think it's never possible to objectively reason, though it's a good exercise to undertake for some uses.

Birkerts makes it a point to bring up the current research on brains, thinking, and different kinds of experience, but he stops short of what fMRI has been showing, which is that the skill of reading is a hat trick that makes marks on paper call up sounds in one's head that add up to words and sentences -- a rhizomatous skill. That is, it amounts to the brain inventing its own way to do this with a little prompting and a lot of motivation. No two people read in quite the same way because no two people's brains are performing in quite the same way "between rhizomes." These may or may not correspond to actual structures: hippocampus, lateral pre-frontal cortex, spindle cells or what have you. Evidently some people do it one way and others do it another. No doubt someone is trying to figure out the possibilities even as you read this.

But then Birkerts makes an important second step. Simply reading words is one thing, entering an experience is another, and that's what he means by "the novel." Humans are uniquely equipped to step into the experience of another being. I was never so conscious of this as when trying to reach my younger brother who had trauma to his forehead that took that skill away from him. He no longer read fiction, but enjoyed turning the pages of the encyclopedia, reading entries and looking up now and then to tell us facts. He was capable of recounting long strings of events, mostly from the plots of television shows, but had no sense of how they added up. Birkerts says "narration is sequence that claims significance."

When one reads something that really reaches into one's gut, the reader is sharing experience with the writer quite regardless of plot lines or facts and responding to the significance, the meaning. The question of whether it really happened or not doesn't matter. Sometimes even the skill of the writer in terms of "mimesis," the management of description, dialogue, event, evocation, doesn't matter a whole lot -- one still has the inner experience of sharing the mind of the writing person. Birkerts suggests it is partly a matter of being focused, of suspending disbelief in order to enter someone else's world. THIS, he suggests, is what the Internet does not support, even erodes. "Fiction" allows contemplation, the imaginative consideration of possibilities which Birkerts rather wonderfully calls "the ignition to inwardness," but Internet analysis opposes this. Instead, it sets up the cry of "hoax" and enters the hermeneutics of suspicion, a matter of bookkeeping.

I think the next step is "revanchist." (I really DO like big words -- it just means revenge.) The person who cannot kindle contemplation knows something is missing, just as my brother did, but can't get hold of what it is and begins to feel that someone has stolen something, though it might never have existed. So then, paranoia. A missing education? A refusal of people to love him or her? Not enough money?

"Big Bad Love" is an exploration of consciousness: a man who has been badly traumatized and is thrashing around in that biological way that desperate people do: drinking, violence, endless driving -- but also by writing. Not just saying he wants to write but actually sitting there at his little typewriter and clicking away. Because this is a movie, it can take us into the metaphorical/poetic mode of operation in his head. I loved it when his typewriter turned into a small piano, which is often my own fantasy. I take his search for publication to be a trope: being published stands for achieving meaning. It means some stranger's sensibility has kindled and extends love. His enormous strength is the ability to focus on writing, mailing out the manuscripts, and opening up the rejection letters which he pins to the bathroom wall with game darts. In other words he keeps right on in spite of the excremental put-downs from the uncomprehending.

So how does he come to meaning? He could have asked his ex-wife, who is a nurse. It's the old rabbinical trick of the person obsessing about the loss of her child until he tells her to go with a cup begging house-to-house for a cup of soil from a family untouched by loss. Or in a slightly different way, the man who was so upset about having no shoes until he saw someone with no feet. That is, it finally gets through to him that the meaning of life is to keep living, risking, protecting, making contact, sharing and creating. But it is a quiet epiphany. He doesn't have to go celebrating. The change is one of depth.

So now I can explain that major division between those who loved the movie and those who hated the movie. It is the division between "fiction" readers and "Internet" readers, those who contemplate and those who score.

# IS "THE GLADIATOR" AN ALPHA MALE?

Though I don't have television, I have not escaped the images from Pakistan and Afghanistan of tall robed men in turbans with full beards and flashing eyes. Neither have I missed the strong dark jaws or penetrating blue eyes of the Marines. We are getting a full dose of the military version of the Alpha Male. Which is about where you'd expect to find Alphas. The concept comes from wolf packs where one wolf dominates all the others. The poor Beta wolves, plural, must wait until Alpha weakens or they grow stronger and can "take" him in a fight. (Actually it's more complicated than that, but this is the way the concept is seen.)

**TheRawness.com** takes on today's meat market among the employed, generally mainstream, mild-mannered, middle-class American men, those who aren't so poor that they live in the shadows nor so rich that they can do as they please. He's been spending some time trying to analyze how Alpha and Beta play into this and today he came to his conclusion. First he lists two fallacies. One is that everything good a modern man can be must represent an alpha trait. (The report card interpretation.) The other is that everything that represents an alpha trait must represent something good for a modern man to be. (The prescription interpretation.)

**"The point of this whole series has been to point out why these fallacies are actually fallacies, especially for middle-class men. For middle-class men in modern society, the best response to take in many scenarios is often the beta response. And for middle-class men in modern society, many alpha traits can also be extremely counterproductive and even self-destructive."**

"RickyRaw," the blogger, points out that in capitalist, democratic, developed, monogamous circumstances, the Alpha qualities of imposing order, suppressing violence even with the use of violence, making CEO decisions, and so on are delegated to what he calls *"Alpha proxies"* like legislators and the police. Protections, provisions for the needy, and so on are delegated to the state or the church or other organizations. And yet we insist on maintaining the myth that an Alpha male is one who defies all this. This causes what he calls *"Alpha Dissonance."*

I just watched the companion DVD to *"Gladiator"* that is three hours long and explains how the movie was made. (I'm not changing the subject.) It began with **David Franzoni** reading about Rome, which seems to catch the fancy of a lot of modern men, and he had creds from *"Amistad"* which he cashed in with **Stephen Spielberg**. Then he went to **Ridley Scott** with a print of a painting by **Jean-Léon Gérôme**, *Pollice Verso ("Thumbs Down")*, which was very much in the lush style of **Alma-Tadema**, depicting a grisly moment in the Coliseum when an opponent is down flat and the Emperor is signaling to kill him. Very Alpha.

Now I need a little schematic invented by **Athol Kay**, one of those quadrant charts like the Johari Window.

http://www.marriedmansexlife.com/2010/01/little-more-on-alpha-and-beta-male.html

| Alpha Traits Yes<br>Beta Traits No<br><br>"Alpha Male"<br>Bad Boy | Alpha Traits Yes<br>Beta Traits Yes<br><br>"Gamma Male"<br>Married Game |
|---|---|
| Alpha Traits No<br>Beta Traits No<br><br>"Omega Male"<br>Total Loser | Alpha Traits No<br>Beta Traits Yes<br><br>"Beta Male"<br>Nice Guy |

Franzoni is one of those men who understands that there's a time to be Alpha and a time to be Beta. **Ridley Scott** is a movie director: movie directors are Alphas. I don't care how they dominate (carefully), they DO dominate. So Franzoni just slipped this print to him and Ridley was on board.

Then it got interesting. There was no script, just an idea. Franzoni went to work but ran aground and brought in **John Logan**. Again later, they got stuck and brought in **William Nicholson**. All of these men were writers, all were seriously intelligent, all knew what they were doing, and they did not put each other down. (Gammas?) They went for the core ideas: this is a movie about a gladiator. Okay. His family has been destroyed. Okay. He's going to kill the bad emperor. Okay. But it's been done before. More thought. Finally, the epiphany was that this was a man who just wanted to go home. He was violent, he was ruthless, he was dominating, but in the end he just wanted to go home. The fact that "home" turned out to be the Elysian Fields was all the more poignant. Ridley Scott understood at once. Women love this movie so much because The Gladiator was a Gamma Male.

There were two men in this cast who didn't really get Alpha Dissonance, who totally bought the idea that real men do their own stunts, drink like fish, have their own way, and so on. One was **Oliver Reed**, who had played the acting game that way all his life, but only on his own time. When he was on the set, he was a dependable Beta. Mostly. But his Alphaness killed him before the picture was finished. He died of a heart attack in a bar one Sunday.

The other person was **Russell Crowe**, who kept trying to rewrite the script himself. He just felt he WAS an Alpha, therefore, he knew what the character was all about and he would just be Australian about it. Evidently he has not resolved this Alpha Dissonance in the years since and Alpha Proxies have had to slow him down now and then.

The perfect Beta male in this movie was played by **Djimon Hounson**, drawn into a larger and larger part until he got the final word. In early versions he was only a buddy, just as formidable as a gladiator, but nurturing and protective of his friend as we understand black tribal people to be. What choice do they have when only white people can be Alphas? It's a useful racism. (Cicero is also an honorable Beta.) And poor weak Commodos is an Omega who has been born into a role for an Alpha, as his sister could be, and has let his insufficiency deeply corrupt him. So the Alpha Proxies, the senators, are willing to help knock him out.

See how useful this stuff is? Excellent pot lifters for moving concepts around. And we surely need to work on this. The comments were appalling. One man insisted that only a sociopath had the balls to be a true Alpha and offered himself as an example. Most of them obsessed about getting enough sex. One reader suggested a new series analyzing women and another thought (evidently seriously) that such a series would have to be written by a lesbian. (Maybe he was trying to think of the word for "feminist.")

As a humanist, I suggest an Alien from another galaxy be invited in. But I was encouraged that a commenter on Athol Kay's blog suggested that Jean Luc Picard was the perfect strategic Alpha, willing to play Beta and Gamma when the situation was right. Never an Omega.

# VENUS: A Review

Last night's movie was *"Venus,"* in which a tottering **Peter O'Toole** relates to a teenaged girl bluffing her way along because she really has no idea at all what's going on. Her only source of nurturing seems to be Top Ramen noodles and beer. The main strategy of those in charge of her is rejection and attempted domination (quite useless). The O'Toole character ("Maurice") is a sensualist. He loves this girl ("Jessie") for her young peach of a body. Why would he love her mind? What mind?

The miracle is that Jessie, in spite of herself, begins to stir as Maurice escorts her through galleries, theatres, and ideas. In the end it's fair exchange, a literal end that Maurice doesn't face alone and for Jessie an end that is really a beginning. Maurice is ecstatic over the smell of Jessie's neck, shamelessly avid for the sight of her golden and naked against pink sheets, but he never crosses whatever boundaries Jessie imposes, an entirely new experience for her and one she experiments with, concentrating, never offended by Maurice's age, unlike most of the reviewers, who automatically consider old men obscene and offensive. (They never think of old women at all.)

This movie was written by **Hanif Koreishi** rather quickly, he explains, and was one of those scripts that just unfolded organically, partly through the casting. (I love watching these explanations afterwards.) The original idea was a sort of Brit grumpy old men inspired by the little coffee shop where a few geezers were regulars, but then they somehow became actors with those amazing Shakespeare and BBC repertory company backgrounds and overtones as rich as cello concertos. As much as they might grieve over lost powers (about the only parts left for them to play are corpses) they can glory in their pasts and the solidarity of the stage world. Every shot in this film is a potential Old Master painting: framed, composed, elegant and eloquent.

For me, this is a sort of been-there-done-that tale since my primary love affair was as a 21-year-old with a 47-year-old. It wasn't quite the same thing because for a few brief years we were the same age, my powers on the rise and his in decline, but this film comes much closer to a true exchange than so many of the **Woody Allen** dirty-old-man formulations that ridicule and demean all concerned. One reviewer of *"Amazing Aphrodite"* thought **Woody Allen** was repulsively old at sixty. Allen is no O'Toole, but in real life at least one young woman didn't find him that repulsive.

My personal reaction to this film (and what is not a personal reaction to a film when you watch a DVD alone with cats in your own front room?) is even more warm after watching the **von Trier** *"Dancer in the Dark,"* which is bleak to the point of unbearability. At the moment in various sources von Trier's latest, *"Antichrist,"* is being discussed as over-the-top, too misogynistic to be taken seriously -- too ugly, too violent, too depression-obsessed, and too male-punishing-female for modern society. The *NYTimes* review is more dismissive than horrified reactions in *Salon* and *Slate*. It's telling that two of von Trier's former actress heroines have refused to be in any of his subsequent films.

So the *"Scent of a Woman"* tone of "Venus" is certainly welcome. It's as though we've had to reach back to an earlier age to recover the ordinary erotics of daily life, instead of the constant attempt to be more shocking, darker, more gruesome, as a way to feel SOMETHING ANYTHING. But in the end the result of extremes is like the survivor of torture in *"Rendition,"* a near-zombie. All the torment blurs together and there is no enlightenment.

*"Venus"* is not in any sense misogynist, though it recognizes the hardship that erotic narcissism can impose on others. **Vanessa Redgrave** provides the counterbalance to the ignorant young girl and to the blithe greed of Maurice, who so often makes a fool of himself. Vanessa's just as old, just as eloquent, just as wise, and quite forgiving, but she, as well as the girl, has a clear sense of boundaries and makes Maurice stay on his own side. Her comfort comes from cats. And he can forget seeing the children he deserted, though they are beyond grown-up. At Maurice's inevitable funeral, the wife meets the young woman in a lovely scene. Now Vanessa is dressed in a black velvet turban and a smashing rooster tail feather collar, nearly Elizabethan, and she understands completely what has happened -- finds nothing requiring forgiveness, accepts the young woman as a protegee of her own. Jessie will be able to learn from that now.

The geezers of Valier mostly don't have such rich pasts and the young women like Jessie will never give them the time of day unless they're relations. I passed one of these local beauties in the grocery store the other day, looking like a pole dancer with her long streaked hair, her tight jeans and high-heels, giving off the crocodilian aura of an opportunist. If an old guy had a lot of money, maybe they would give him the time of day. The hunger for money and status will soon take them out of here.

But why does **von Trier** always torture women that are more fawn than reptile? Is it a version of "crush" porn, the kind the Supreme Court is thinking about at the moment? Is there something about innocent devotion that makes the young irresistible to predators? And what allows these women to be abused? Society? The models they see in movies?

The name of the screenwriter, **Hanif Koreishi**, echoed for me **Kent Haruf** and his novel about two old rural bachelors who decide to shelter a young pregnant woman. I once got into a big argument over whether any old men ever do anything selfless or helpful, whether they aren't always smelly beasts who must have their own way. I defended old men with the Haruf novel as my evidence. It could happen here. But that's not the same thing as this film, which is a kind of mutual redemption, each person leading from strength and achieving in intimacy a mutual respect.

# A MURDER/SUICIDE: TRAGEDY OR TRANSCENDENT?

Clearly the two deaths were a murder/suicide. There was a witness and a camera was running. He was a famous warrior but showed no symptoms of PTSD, even though he had witnessed and participated in many Middle East atrocities, often perpetrated by the leader of his own nation. It seemed that he was just so in love with the action of the battles that he was willing to ignore the victims. Just the same, he was a leading philanthropist who gave away fortunes to the poor.

She was the perpetrator, in spite of long service in religious orders working with hospitals. This was where she got her knowledge of poisons, which let her choose a painless sort of death for herself and her lifelong lover, who -- according to his best friend and fighting companion -- was reconciled to the death on grounds that he didn't wish to age anymore. He considered himself elderly though he was barely fifty, if that.

He was handsome, a hunk. Well, maybe a Big Lug. His friend was an even Bigger Lug, but he didn't understand what was going on. The killer was religious, or so she claimed. At the end she stated she loved this guy more than God. She also refused to mourn him, which is a religious duty. More than that, she was Catholic which prohibits both murder and suicide. Just not Holy Wars, though they cause both.

The motive seems quite mysterious but the facts are very clear. They've been more or less known for centuries, but not quite this take. It's **Robin Hood**, the 1976 version with **Sean Connery** and **Audrey Hepburn**. Robin has come back from the Crusades where **Richard the Lion-Hearted** had become besotted with violence and dominance to the point where Robin wanted out. Released by Richard's death, he returns home where everything has gone to pieces. It's not so much a case of Robin feeling old as the constant reminders that nothing is as it once was when his sheer vitality carried him along. Marian has become a devoted (but cursing) abbess (management), reconciled to the way things are, though she has tried suicide in the past. We see the scars on her wrist and she freely admits it. So the precursors are there. But she is quickly drawn back into Robin's orbit. So are others.

Everyone wants the past except the Sheriff of Nottingham, who is not a bad sort in this incarnation. (Almost all the main characters are played by actors whose lives echo the figures they are assigned. This one is **Robert Shaw**. **Richard Harris** is King Richard, the Lion-Hearted who becomes a bit of a hyena.)

This story has been repeatedly inhabited by remarkable actors and reinterpreted partly by the choice of characters, the plot emphasis, but most of all by the casting. I see there is a new one coming up next year, directed by **Ridley Scott**, which appears to be *Gladiator II*: same smoking forest, same wolf on the trail, same **Russell Crowe**. This time Maid Marian is **Cate Blanchett** and I see in the little preview trailer that they have used the becoming-cliche gesture of one lover putting a hand over the other lover's face. Is he obliterating her identity or memorizing it? All we know for sure is that it's about identity.

For most people, **Erroll Flynn** IS Robin Hood (1938). His Maid Marian was **Olivia deHavilland**. The sex was mostly in the sub-text, since "in like Flynn" is a phrase that originated about this time during a trial in which Flynn was accused of having seduced a girl in a shower and the whole jury trooped down to the shower in question since it was rather small and Flynn (reluctantly) said it would have been an impossible feat. **Basil Rathbone** was Sir Guy of Gisborne, an adversary who doesn't appear in "*Robin and Marian*." **Claude Rains** was Prince John and **Ian Hunter** was King Richard.

The movie was made at an "interesting" time between the end of the Great Depression and the beginning of WWII. Economics and heroism were of great interest. The first director was replaced by **Michael Curtiz**, born in 1888 in Budapest and more famous for "*Casablanca*." He often worked closely with Flynn and brought Flynn into the picture.

Of the many other versions of Robin Hood, **Kevin Costner**'s is the most forgettable and maybe he ought to be grateful. His Maid Marian was **Mary Elizabeth Mastrantonio**. No one wanted to stop thinking about Dunbar in "*Dances with Wolves*" which was Costner's immediately preceding film. "*Robin Hood, Prince of Thieves*" was released in 1991, a strange time. A rising social consciousness didn't seem to know where to go. Like Costner.

"*Robin and Marian*" (1976) captures an elegiac tone at a time when the great WWII heroes were fading. To us in 2010 both Connery and Hepburn don't look that old. To us, maybe forty or even fifty is the new thirty. Hepburn and Shaw checked out early, but we've watched Connery and Harris age. Now we know what a graceful and hearty old age looks like, and we also know what a frail dissipation-riddled old age looks like. Both are still onscreen, Connery still a romantic hero and maybe even the true King of Scotland. He still IS James Bond.

I had thought that maybe I could use this movie as a contrast to "*Unforgiven*" or even "*Gran Torino*," since Eastwood is also a mega-personality. In "*Unforgiven*" he prevails -- collects his reward and moves his family to San Francisco where they thrive. In "*Gran Torino*" he chooses suicide, though violent. (Robin had no choice but had a painless death.) It looks to me as though the two movies are advocating self-extinction not because THEY were aging, but because they didn't like the times. (English Bob -- **Richard Harris** again -- goes out fighting, but he's not offered as a role model.)

*Robin and Marian* is a beautifully seductive film, as poignant as the three apples rotting on the windowsill. Our feelings are so engaged that it's hard to think about the actual facts. Hepburn makes euthanasia seem transcendent, a religious act justified by love. "I love you more than God," she says to Robin. A heresy. Would you have accepted this outcome if Marian had been *Mary Elizabeth Mastrantonio?* I wonder what **Cate Blanchett** will do.

# "GLITTERING PRIZES" vs. "LOVE IN A COLD CLIMATE"

The first paragraph of a review of *Lucinella* by **Kati Nolfi** for the "*Book Slut*" blog.

*"Artists are cherished and reviled for their bad behavior. They transgress where normal people cannot. In Lore Segal's Lucinella, a thrilling experimental novella first published in 1976 and now reissued by Melville House's Contemporary Art of the Novella series, New York poets are a competitive and shallow bunch. The bad behavior in Lucinella is the social kind; while there's some indiscriminate fucking, there's no homicide or drug addiction. The poets are preoccupied with who's who, who's where, what they're writing, who they're doing. They are writers, but they are not self-sacrificing ascetics as some assume artists must be. They would sacrifice each other for a speaking engagement or publication; an editor's career is described as "standing on your writers' shoulders, alternatively with your foot on one or another of their necks." You could call the relationships symbiotic or more accurately, opportunistic. They search for meaning, order, fame, and transcendence in dowdyish party scenes of empty fabulousness and joyless desperation. But then each success proves insignificant and fuels the search for the next one."*

This is a pretty apt summary of "*The Glittering Prizes.*" Now I've watched **Nancy Mitford**'s "*Love in a Cold Climate*" or rather the BBC version by **Debora Moggash**. The two series make an interesting comparison because both are fictionalized autobiography, they are about post-war periods after WWI ("Love in. . ." filmed in 2002) and after WWII ("Glittering Prize" filmed in 1975) but the actual films were made in reverse order. "Love in" follows the progress of related women (the famous Mitford sisters) and "Glittering Prize" follows a small group of Cambridge students (Raphael's cohort), who are at first considered the very epitome of the best and by the end mocked as stuck and old-fashioned. (I'd say the end was a lot more convincing than the beginning.) Both are about ways of life that are pretty much gone now: the over-educated brilliant young genius (most of the plot rests on the shoulders of **Tom Conti** who plays a Jewish semi-intruder -- more **Dustin Hoffman** than **Al Pacino**) in an abrasive and competitive world. "Love in .." is about the uneducated but high-spirited young women of the landed gentry gone goofy by inbreeding or something, who somehow seem destined to shine without awards.

I cannot conceal that I enjoyed "*Love in a Cold Climate*" far more than "*Glittering Prizes.*" There are some obvious reasons, like the fact that "Love in. . ." is about women. Some people would mind that the young ones are slender and bright with bouncing pointy breasts (Didn't people wear bras in those days?) but I don't. It was easy to identify with their energy. The eccentrics in "Love in. . ." are played masterfully by terrifically talented and experienced English actors. The "Glittering" actors are very young, though they would later become stalwarts.

Maybe some of my dislike of "Glittering" comes from knowing the types all too well. Didn't the NU geniuses start out very much this way? The U of C geniuses were like this, at least the ones I knew, which were the least brilliant since the truly brilliant ones were hard at work somewhere, the source of their genius. But the daughters of the landed gentry are far enough in the past to romanticize, even if these girls are not quite far enough back to be **Jane Austen** heroines or even the cynical women of **Edith Wharton**. Think "The House of Eliot." It does help to introduce the Paris factor, where men escape the deadly English love of drafty castles and bird hunting. The impossible and goofy father in this version **(Alan Bates)** is more lovable than most, since his violence after WWI is mostly a matter of writing an enemy's name on a piece of paper and putting it in a deadly drawer, which he believes will kill them within the year.

The biggest difficulty with "Glittering" took me a while to figure out. Even though **Frederic Raphael** had considerable experience with movies, this series is done with stage technique. Raphael writes quips suitable for throwing to the far reaches of the auditorium. The actors are stage actors who react broadly, hold for laughs, and even mug as though they were dozens of feet away. And most of all, the camera works like a Fifties television camera with very little editing, none of it particularly artful though there are clever angles over the tops of furniture or around corners. Everything moves way too slowly. And the furniture, etc., is not from a particularly fortunate period IMHO. The women are simply inexplicable: they don't seem capable of transparency or even manageability, simply taking abrupt turns without much warning except that the patterns are predictable. ("Wife becomes bored and turns to a career." "Career woman abandons all for family.") The whole thing seems to be mapped more than motivated.

So my premise is that this movie series, even though it was written by an Oscar winner (which sits glittering in the background of one episode) is actually clinging to a past medium and that makes it deadly. It is an auto that acts like a buggy. When I went to *imdb.com* to see if others remarked on it, I found something quite funnily transparent. There were comments, very similar, all saying how wonderful and topnotch everything was, and begging/commanding that such a treasure be released on DVD at once. Clearly, the troupe had united their fans, friends and probably family in a successful effort to get this series "out there." But it was a case of "be awful careful what you wish for, because you might get it." It might have been better to have just remembered how brilliant it was.

Since the Mitford story is easier to grasp and, to be honest, much funnier since the fun doesn't depend on smart talk but rather on essentially impossible situations, it survives the passage of time. But also, the editing is brisk, the sets cannot be topped (the great houses of England and a few excellent places in Paris) and the characters look out at the world as much as they look inward.

# PARIS J'TAIME! A Review & a Suggestion

*"Paris, Je t'aime!"* is great to watch on a DVD because you can stop between the episodes to savor and reflect. Eighteen vignettes on the theme of love, each limited to five minutes and assigned to a specific neighborhood of Paris, and all directed by exceptionally outstanding directors using actors they love and admire, this anthology is remarkably lovable. Usually projects this grand fall flat on their faces.

Not that everyone likes every piece -- in fact, the comments on imdb.com are interesting more because they are from such different points of view than that they are particularly insightful. Some directors were being utterly practical: for instance, *"Tuileries"* was shot underground in a subway station so that shooting wouldn't be interrupted by rain -- as *"Quais de Seine"* was. But the results were totally different as well: *"Tuileries"* was directed by the **Coen** brothers with their usual violent, sexy action and weirdo characters caught up in impossible situations. They managed to refer to the famous gallery without marching us up and down the spaces, dollying past paintings.

**Gurinder Chadha** (You have to be really into the global scene to know her, I guess) was the director interrupted by weather, but she kept the focus on her delicate and idealistic cross-cultural love-at-first-sight scene. **Gus van Sant**'s bit, *"La Marais"* was a sort of same-sex version but when one of the couple took off running as fast as he could, I was unclear whether he was running AFTER the interested party, AWAY from him, or just running to use up energy he had been suppressing. Maybe the ambiguity was the point.

Two episodes depended on knowing the actors and both were for older watchers who could enjoy the reflexivity. One was *"Quartier Latin"* with **Ben Gazzara** and **Gena Rowlands**, waited on by **Gerard Depardieu** in a pleasant little cafe while they sparred over a divorce, clearly way overdue. Their ambivalence over each other is matched by our own ambivalence at seeing beloved actors, but so old! So old! Then **Bob Hoskins** plays off against **Fanny Ardent** in the Pigalle, the most English actor ever -- squat and pugnacious -- against the most French actor ever -- elegance embodied.

There was love for children: **Juliette Binoche**, a bereaved mother, is given one last reunion with her dead son while **Willem Defoe**, a horseman of death portrayed as a cowboy, stands by. In another tale largely in the subway, an immigrant mother wakes her child and leaves him in a nursery, singing him a little song, then travels to her job as a nanny where she sings the same song to the child she is caring for.

Some tales were nutty, one in a traditional way with two white-faced mimes who are parents to a sturdy little boy, and one in a goofy frantic hair-dresser extravaganza that's philosophically fuzzy, but fun just the same. And the obligatory vampire tale with the reddest blood ever catches up "Frodo Baggins" in another unreal adventure: Frodo lives...forever.

The one I loved the most was very simple: an immigrant parking attendant, **Seydou Boro**, sees a beautiful girl -- love at first sight! Then later he gets into a quarrel on the street, through no fault of his own,and is fatally stabbed. The girl, **Aïssa Maïga**, returns as the responding EMT. He begs her to have a cup of coffee with him "later," but she already knows there will be no "later." Nevertheless, she asks someone to bring two cups of coffee, in case he lives long enough to share them with her. He does not. **Oliver Schmitz** is the director, a South African, who tells his story with great simplicity and tenderness. The actors are black. I don't know about Schmitz.

The wind-up story is the love affair between a solitary tourist and Paris itself. **Margo Martinda**, an actress you'll recognize but not be able to name, is Carol in the "*14ème Arrondissement*", walking, walking, walking which she doesn't mind a bit since normally she's a letter carrier in Denver. Nor does she mind being alone in a city full of lovers -- she loves her two dogs and will be happy to get home to them in spite of this "affair" in Paris.

The potential for using this DVD is enormous. It is a course in cinema all of itself. It gives lots of material for a philosophical discussion of love. One could analyze style and cinema tricks like making vampire blood practically glow in the dark or the mimes putter through the streets without moving anything but their feet, which are blurred with speed. One could address nationality: French, English, American, Islam, South African -- or class.

But what I think would be most fun would be to divide one's own town into neighborhoods and write a story for each of them. Maybe I'll try it. In McKinley, Montana, the imaginary town that's geographically on a website: *McKinleyMontana.com*. A railroad neighborhood, a growing suburb, the mall, the main street, and so on. Or maybe Valier: along the lake, on a modest historic street, in a block of old houses versus a block of new houses, the "field" of grain bins, the trash roll-off.

Or how about a series of stories on the rez. I did one in terms of time, *"Twelve Blackfeet Stories."* Now maybe I'll do one for each town, maybe an old-timer town like Heart Butte and then a "young tourist" town like St. Mary. Moccasin Flats would have to be a memory piece. East Glacier a plan-for-the-future piece?

Or it would be possible to write a story for each "arrondissement." I think I'll try it: a fishing story by Willow Creek interrupted by a drunk; a one-hundred-year old Blackfeet woman at the IHS hospital, so white and clean it looks like the inside of a spaceship, and a young nurse who is slow to realize that this old woman is her blood ancestor. An espresso barista in the big old concrete tipi who is fascinated by a young black man who arrives in a Porsche, hoping that maybe HE's Blackfeet. A playground drama on one of the elementary school grounds. A library discovery at the high school, maybe a note found in one of the books that was written by his grandfather. See how easy it is?

# LOVERS AND MARRIAGES: A Double/Triple Review

I have a Chinese girl friend from grade school and high school. I went to the Senior Prom with her and her fiancee and was a bridesmaid in her wedding. Their fiftieth anniversary is coming up but she doesn't want me to post any photos or to talk about her, so I'll do it covertly by reviewing two movies. Just let me say that they're fiercely intent on being assimilated immigrants at the same time that they embrace everything in their Chinese heritage. Their understanding of American culture is, well, Baptist.

The two movies are *"Two Lovers"* and *"A Good Woman."*

*"A Good Woman"* probably ought to have kept the original title -- or at least a closer echo -- since it is an admirable remake of *"Lady Windermere's Fan,"* the **Oscar Wilde** stage classic. As it turned out, the Italians (where the movie was filmed) informed them (too late!) that "a good woman" is an Italian euphemism for a prostitute, which is a rather sharp comment on a plot that addresses the differences between marriage for high ideals and romance (enabled by money) and marriage for opportunity (money) and, well, friendship. There are two young married people: the young woman (**Scarlet Johanson** who was 19 at the time and not quite famous yet) is pursued by a handsome young man who wishes nothing more than an adventure. The young husband seems to have been captured by an older woman who is draining money from his checkbook, which has been her modus operandi over the years. This is in the context of a group of Brit ex-pats scurrying through the Mediterranean pleasure spots in the early Thirties.

Here's a relevant quote from *"Two-Spirit People"* (what a useful book!): *". . . Southall's reference to Banton's contention that "high moral density is associated with small population groups where everyone knows everyone else so that deviance in role performance by one person affects all the rest."* I like that phrase "high moral density," which I think refers to consensus rather than idealistic aspirations. The deviant in this case is the innocent and absolutely faithful young bride, who is a pigeon among the cats. But is it? Is she really the "good" woman in question? If you set Oscar Wilde loose in such a circumscribed community, he wields his verbal scalpel tellingly, but not without compassion. This movie reminds some of the similar portraits of the Brit ex-pat community in Kenya. (Has anyone written anything useful about post-colonial theory among ex-pats?)

The setting is Amalfi, impossibly, blissfully gorgeous with villas and ancient churches perched on cliffs overlooking the sea. Italian priests were kept busy denying access when they found out the original story was by Oscar Wilde and one scurvy captain played blackmail by simply sailing off with the yacht that was a set until more money was paid. But the places were so elegantly graceful that practically no set dressing was necessary except tons of silk flowers since they were shooting in the middle of winter. If there were no sound at all, one could just drift in the dream setting, unaware that the actors were freezing to death in their bare, beaded, chiffon gowns. Sometimes their noses are a little pink.

The conclusion is the best possible from the point of view of me, the scriptwriter, the director, the producer and probably the BBC repertory stalwarts. That is, the older woman (**Helen Hunt**) is found by a man (**Tom Wilkinson**) with plenty of money and much the same sort of (ahem) experienced past, who is capable of relating in a real way with a practical philosophy. The "sadder but wiser girl is the girl for him." They literally fly off into the sunset, another meltingly paradisical scene.

The other movie, called *"Two Lovers,"* could not be more different. Written from the life experience of the director/screenwriter who grew up in Brighton Beach, a smaller part of the New York complex, the movie opens with **Joaquin Phoenix** committing suicide by dropping off a bridge. When he's rescued, he merely walks home, dripping. He's just been jilted, is supposed to be on drugs, and is a great worry to his solid, conventional Jewish parents. He's a pretty good black-and-white photographer who takes grim formal facades of shabby buildings. His parents have found him the perfect wife, who already loves him. But **Gwyneth Paltrow** lives just across the courtyard in the same apartment building. Uh-oh. She's always in a state of crisis, appealing to him for help. He never turns her down, though she gives him the slip and hangs onto her older rich lawyer lover who refuses to leave his family.

It's certainly obvious what he ought to do. It's also obvious why he keeps responding to Gwyneth. There's no sparkling dialogue, no gorgeous villas, no fabulous clothes. Phoenix plods along, heart-driven. He's so earnest and generous, it's hard to be very angry with him. Even the woman his parents chose remains available and forgiving. All we can do is hope this is going to work out as it should. It does. (**Isabella Rossellini** is Phoenix' mother -- how can anyone raised by her go wrong?)

The next movie I saw after these two (I must have been into romances for some reason) was *"Evening,"* which is all about a wedding and the misadventures during it, as recalled on the deathbed of **Vanessa Redgrave**. Her daughter is in the film, so is **Meryl Streep** and her daughter, and so is **Eileen Atkins**, another fab BBC actress who is the "night nurse" but more like "Glinda the Good Witch" as Redgrave sees her. The plot is again regrets and blunders with the general moral that we do the best we can and everyone's life is a mixture of happiness and wretchedness. The house is one of those idyllic Newport places perched on a sea cliff but not quite up to Amalfi grandeur. Good try, but there's a kind of **Edward Hopper** feel to it. It's American Hallmark phony, really. Blowing curtains, fireflies, and and Arrow shirt model who is the lynchpin of the story since for some unknown reason everyone is in love with him.

In the end the moral of all three romances is that you can't hope to have a life into which no rain ever falls, not to say car crashes and even deaths, but you do the best you can and when you look back over a long stretch of years, it will be the good things, the well-loved things that remain in your mind and heart. American Baptist Chinese do this better than anyone else. Confucian Christians have got to be the world's most reliable people, esp. when it comes to family. They don't need fancy scenery, but they appreciate it when they see it. And their marriages last.

FRIDAY, NOVEMBER 28, 2008

# UNEQUAL RELATIONSHIPS

My recent movies seem to be falling into a theme, or maybe a set of interlocked themes: big/little power relationships, power that comes from status, and what happens when big loses status and slides to little. The movies are *"Callas Forever,"* *"Country Life"* (an Australian interpretation of Chekhov's *"Uncle Vanya,"* and an episode of the Inspector Lynley series, *"If Wishes Were Horses."* I'll work through them backwards.

But first, we have a major social conviction that relationships should be equal, not just under the law or in terms of citizenship but as person-to-person, especially in intimate relationships. And yet I can hardly think of any relationships around me that are truly equal. Besides that, we seem to have major problems with the professional classes, who are supposed to be bigger than the rest of us in terms of power and knowledge. I mean doctors, lawyers, ministers and other roles that are meant to award power to people who will use it for good, who will be restrained by their peers (who ARE equal-to-equal), and who make a clear "profession" that this is their intention. **Dr. Nuland**, who writes powerfully about doctors, suggests that today's doctors are seriously undermined by the loss of their association with religiously endorsed moral requirements such as compassion and freedom from corruption. Those of us who loved *"The Infinite Mind"* on NPR have been sickened (iatrogenically) by **Dr. Fred Goodwin's** recent exposure as accepting a million dollar payment from a manufacturer of psychotropic drugs. No need to point out the many, many other convictions of high officials for low behavior.

(The rest of this is riddled with what *imdb.com* calls "spoilers.")

The premise of the Inspector Lynley series of BBC mysteries is that the Inspector himself is high class, highly educated, handsome, and well-aware of it, which means he is also arrogant, high-handed, smirking, and sometimes blind to ordinary humans. His sidekick, a tiny but intense woman (I always think of **Sharon Butala**), is lower-class, inclined to ignore procedure, pig-headed, and far more open to the run of ordinary humans. The idea is that though these two are unequal in rank and background, their inequalities mesh to create a synergy that solves mysteries. The idea is a powerful one, but it appears to be quite a challenge to script writers.

In *"If Wishes Were Horses"* another superior being (a forensic psychologist or "profiler" -- a handsome white man, of course) is murdered. A serial bonker, it turns out that he has even taken a turn with Lynley's wife far in the past. Said wife is also a "profiler" who seems not have had a very good insight into this murder victim when she was his student. There's a second murder and then a third, if you count the loss of a fetus in a car accident. Possibly a fourth if you count the alert little sergeant who throws herself into the line of fire to protect a murderer while Lynley stands by, looking noble. That's the closing, so we don't know whether she survives.

The general rule with BBC scripts is that the perp is the least-likely possibility and so she is: a beautiful female doctor who wants power over the docile wife of the dead man. (Also, not incidentally, his estate which includes a rather fabulous stone house with huge window/doors in the front.) The dead man is an abuser and a likely candidate for killer is his bitter but cheerfully realistic first wife, who is no longer docile. She has learned from her afflictions and anyway, she's Irish. She'll take a beating only up to a point -- then she wants compensation. (The actress also played the long-suffering wife of *"Cracker,"* who is still my fav BBC forensic psycher.) And she gets her reward since the second wife (but possibly thousandth boinkee) has been found out in her over-liberal acceptance of "comfort" from the beautiful lesbian doctor. There are a lot of smart comments all through this episode about people patronizing, underestimating, disregarding, and disbelieving -- but also about the people who accept such treatment. The neediness seems to be part of the problem.

*"Country Life"* revolves around two powerful men: the **Sam Elliot** character who is also a doctor, and Voysey, the uncle who has been a popular reviewer in England, now just returned with his new and elegant wife. It's another of the post-war chaos times (1919) with everyone trying to preserve their status and prospects while realizing that the rules have been very much changed. The girl who would previously have been idle is now a true working partner of the ranch, the man who was previously respected is now a has-been and the woman who threw in her lot with him in hopes of safety is now going over the cliff with him. To her credit, she sticks with the bargain. The uncle who runs the ranch despairs, but in fact is supporting everyone else, which he now begins to realize. The doctor ruefully rides on his way, his integrity a bit compromised but his compassion intact. What's interesting is that on reflection it is the tough old cook, played by **Googie Withers**, who has the real power. She sees it all and sets the schedule as well as the table.

*"Callas Forever"* is a reincarnation of a Diva, the near-definition of a powerful person. But she doesn't guard her power-source, her voice, and when it goes, she loses everything including **Onassis**. **Jeremy Irons** has a scheme for restoring her reputation by dubbing her previously glorious voice onto new film footage, notably *"Carmen."* Since this movie is made by **Zefferelli**, who knew **Callas**, it is gorgeous and knowing. This group of show-biz people might seem careless and corrupt in their relationships, and yet they stand by each other and preserve their equality. **Callas,** in the end, decides the project is an unworthy deception and cancels. (In real life she died not long afterwards.)

Artistic community can be quite vicious, but at its best it's more than community: it's family. Maybe because they work so directly with human psychic qualities, artist friends seem a better wager than business friends -- unless they are too mixed together, which often happens. The business parasites who profit from artists are the most corrupt and in our contemporary culture, they are predatory.

Unequal relationships have their roots in the parent-child relationship. I am not alone in beginning to think that American affluent society has betrayed their children by trying to make them "equal" to the parents when the children have neither the means nor the motivation. Instead they become monsters of narcissism in their efforts to find boundaries. But the "low class" has also been pressed so hard to survive that they simply abandon their children, leaving them with a constant craving for some major figure to embrace them. When women were always "little," they were vulnerable to power figures, but now it is the children who struggle, so needy that they will substitute gangs for family.

I agree with Dr. Nuland that the remedy might be a new "religion" that is powerful enough to urge integrity and compassion on our society. But I reject the idea of going back to the too-many-times reconstructed Middle Eastern Abramic patterns. The best I can imagine is a cross between **Obama**-calm and **Dalai Lama**-compassion, but circumstances may be changing so drastically that something entirely new is forming. I hope it hurries. As I age, I become smaller, more at the mercy of doctors.

# THE GIRL IN THE CAFE:

*"The Girl in the Cafe"* was touted as being sort of like *"Lost in Translation,"* which I didn't like. Critics these days can't seem to tell much beyond the most obvious, which is that both movies are about an older guy and a young girl in a hotel world that encourages romantic attachments. But the tone, purpose and enactment of this idea is totally different.

Beyond the plot, *"The Girl in the Cafe"* -- as the more perceptive imdb.com critics noted -- is almost completely dependent on the casting. **Bill Nighy**, surely the most twitchy tall handsome slightly balding actor with fine stage enunciation that we have, meets the earnest Scots serene-but-concerned young woman, **Kelly McDonald**, who is between lives. The man happens to be a gray shadow, what they call these days a "quant" meaning a quantifier, a math guy. His life is no life. He sits down across from "Gina" because there is no other seat in a crowded coffee shop, and their very shyness is a tie between them. Of course, the relationship continues, Nighy's character carefully introducing himself every time he calls, sometimes after just leaving her a few hours earlier. When they come a unexpected step closer together, this guy does an amazing scissors-jump that shows what he's repressing -- except for those escaping twitches.

Then comes the beginning of the real plot. He decides to take his new friend to a G8 summit in Reykjavik where a rich tapestry of land surrounds an absolutely abstract and geometric hotel. We do the usual *"It Happened One Night"* nonsense, suspending disbelief but not as much as the other members of the Brit delegation, who treat Nighy like a slightly dim child -- except for the women who like Gina immediately.

Instead of going shopping with her new friends, Gina settles down to read the presentation papers and watch the televised proceedings. She is not baffled nor daunted, but sees right away that the delegates are supposed to seem to move ahead while preserving the status quo. No actress since **Audrey Hepburn** has so convincingly portrayed the wide-eyed young woman who graciously takes the hand of the big shot and then kindly asks, "Why is it that you're wearing no clothes?" (**Rachel Weitz** in *"The Constant Gardener"* was not so innocent or kind.)

Even the crisis-point is reached in a low key, but the action in this movie happens IN the delegates, who ARE people of conscience, who ARE having trouble sleeping like Bill Nighy, who DO know what they could do, but are afraid of jumping, trained to be obedient no-risk poker players. One has to keep in mind that this is a British television movie and that it was timed to coincide with the real G-8 summit on world poverty in 2005.

In short, this is the plea to the authorities that is mimed at the major formal dinner, where McDonald looks absolutely elegant except that her hair up-do has a tiny bit of a tuft sticking out and her dress IS a teeny bit tight. She doesn't stand and shout or overturn the table. Just quietly and reasonably speaks her piece. And no one interrupts until the end when a hand falls on her shoulder. In fact, the faces of the delegates are the real story. The director says that his theory of England is that the whole place is an iceberg, where the real gravity and weight is unseen beneath. This is palpable as these polite diplomats sit frozen in place at the banquet table.

On imdb.com there are 130 reviews and reactions, maybe evenly split between the cynics who hated it and the idealists who loved it. They would be happy to tear the movie in half, the humorous whimsy of the first part on one side and the challenge to high government on the other, which perhaps tells us more about where society is right now than anything about the movie.

We never see Africa. There's no girl-in-grisly-circumstances as there is in "Constant Gardener" and "Spy Game." We hear some statistics. Humorously told. The girl is removed. All the man can do is accompany her to the airport. And yet everything is changed somehow, a scale has shifted. So this is a morality play, as surely as if it were acted out in medieval times with a guy in a devil suit pitching sinners into a mock hell while declaiming from a traveling wagon stage. And yet it shows that the source of morality is in this quiet tenderness between people. The courage to reach out can be just across a table or across a banquet hall or across the continents.

Iceland was chosen because the real G8 that coincided with this television drama was NOT in Iceland and because Iceland is so removed from our ordinary assumptions and because there's a magical quality about all the mist and the slant-light and the independence of the people. They have a distinctly moral quality as a country, which is why it's hard to see them so hammered by this recent financial collapse.

But the point the movie makes about poverty in Africa is as real right now as it was in 2005 when the movie aired. I get a little impatient about my new way of eating, our whole country is upset about how much food costs, food banks are complaining that the food is going out faster than it's coming in, but we are NOT starving by the millions in this country. Africans are, if they don't die of AIDS first, just as was predicted years ago by the opponents of overpopulation. The most frustrating aspect of it is that we DO have enough food -- we do NOT have the will to get it where it needs to be and we do NOT act strategically to help countries feed themselves. And we've gone into overload about diseases -- our fingers are in our ears.

These two actors, **Kelly MacDonald** and **Bill Nighy**, were also at about this time in their lives shooting "State of Play," which is a masterful long series about the interplay of politics, journalism, and the difficulties of intimacy. It's all lies and secrecy and surprises. In that movie Nighy is the newspaper editor, an old hand, one who sees through all the naughty bits and cuts to the chase, absolutely confident. MacDonald also is in pursuit of the truth, as dedicated, earnest, and intent on asking the key questions as she is in this movie. The director says that the two actors became quite close and I'm sure that's true. The tenderness and careful attention between the two of them is acting, true, but it draws on reality. It's remarkable that so many members of our society resist this kind of connection, both on the personal level and as a society.

# "YES"

My Netflix queue is so long that by the time a film gets to the top of the list and arrives in the mail I've often forgotten why I put it on the list in the first place. Sometimes it's an ad on a previous DVD, sometimes from an article I read in some obscure place -- almost NEVER a result of an automated suggestion. One kind of film I search for is the foreign film explosion of the late Fifties when I was an undergrad in Chicago. In those days one went to a show house or to a film society with a 16mm projector, and endlessly analyzed what one saw. There was no relationship at all to the contemporary habit of piling up on one's sofa to mindlessly kill some time while snacking.

One of the films from those days that hit me square between the eyes was *"Hiroshima, Mon Amour"* by **Marguerite Duras**. It was erotic, of course, because it was about a French woman attending a peace conference in Hiroshima and having an affair with a Japanese man there. The scene of the two of them in the shower together was a revelation to me -- I didn't know you could DO that, much less film it. The real subject, again of course, was how to cross the divides between the sexes, the cultures, the peaceful and the warmongers.

I didn't know that **Sally Potter**'s *"YES"* would be an even more modern and expressionist version of the same classic story. Maybe I only ordered it because the "yes" of Molly Bloom at the end of *"Ulysses"* is one of my favorite sermon devices when I'm in the company of other UU ministers. It always gets a laugh because they know it's about sex and they think no one else knows that -- though it's really about saying yes to life. (Is there a difference? Answer in less than 2,000 words.) Ministers don't get to say "yes" as much as they would like to. They tend to feel the edge of the Apollonian/ Dionysian split because it is sometimes the choice between their vocation and being thrown out. Or used to be.

Until minutes into the film, I didn't realize that everyone was speaking in iambic pentameter -- easily, I might say, like very excellent Shakespearean actors. The cinematography was striking, arty, but not distracting. The framing device of cleaning women "who know more about you than you know about yourself" was entertaining as well as objectifying and a good feminist balance to the almost too mandarin woman doctor.

The Lebanese former doctor-- now putting his surgery to use in a luxury hotel kitchen -- and the female embryologist research doctor are at opposite ends of the experience of life. The Lebanese was right up against the boundary between life and death in terms of violence; the embryologist talks theory about conception while working in a lab where at night the binocular microscopes are sheathed in condom-like plastic. She is the Apollonian, living in a white, sharp-edged, stripped-out house. He is the Dionysian, taking her to a bed of purple, red and orange silk. The actress is cat-faced, pale, blonde, nearly without makeup and certainly without body fat. The actor is dark, tousled, with a noble nose and gallant mustache. We never see her dance; HE dances. It is only after the physical relationship is established that the politics of gender and national culture begin to drive them apart. The final meeting ground is Marxist: Cuba.

For me, absorbing as this film is, the "special features" on the DVD are more important: crucially important. **Sally Potter** is a theatrical polymath: writer, director, dancer, composer, and so on. Her method is that emotional-but-disciplined plunge into the unknowns of theatre as inner-life-made-explicit that was so much at the heart of what we thought was a world revolution in the Sixties and Seventies. Arising out of the peace movement and determination to get to the heart of war -- esp. ambiguous and tortured wars like Vietnam -- as well as tolerance of altered consciousness and ambivalence about asceticism/ eroticism, we wanted to get to the truth. The question was whether we could "handle the truth." Sally hasn't given up this inquiry. I would suggest that too many others have.

When Orpheus descended into hell to try to bring his lover out through the use of art, in his case music, he didn't take any notes. But **Sally Potter** does. She blogs, she forums, she websites, she never hesitates to use electronic communications. I've signed up for her newsletter, just as I've cast off from **Val McDermid**'s. (Val writes ghastly murder mysteries used on "*Wire in the Blood*." I consider her to be perverting something once earnest and pure.)

I know this is the right thing to do, because of this entry by **Sally Potter** on her own website. It is a list of reminders to herself as she started work on a movie called *"Rage."* It is wise enough to guide **Barack Obama** -- maybe he has a similar list.

*The best time to start is now (don't wait)*

*Take responsibility for everything (it saves time)*

*Don't blame anyone or anything (including yourself)*

*Give up being a moviemaker victim (of circumstance, weather, lack of money, mean financiers, vicious critics, greedy distributors, indifferent public, etc.)*

*You can't always choose what happens while you are making a film, but you can choose your point of view about what happens (creative perspective)*

*Mistakes are your best teacher (so welcome them)*

*Turn disaster to advantage (there will be many)*

*Only work on something you believe in (life is too short to practice insincerity)*

*Choose your team carefully and honour them (never speak negatively about your colleagues)*

*Ban the word "compromise" (or the phrase "it will do")*
*(the disappointment in yourself will haunt you later)*

*Be prepared to work harder than anyone you are employing*

*Be ruthless – be ready to throw away your favourite bits (you may well be attached to what is familiar rather than what is good).*

*Aim beyond your limits (and help others to go beyond theirs)*
*(the thrill of the learning curve)*

*When in doubt, project yourself ten years into the future and look back – what will you be proud of having done?*
*(indecision is a lack of the longer view or wider perspective)*

*Practice no waste – psychic ecology – prevent brain pollution*
*(don't add to the proliferation of junk)*

*Be an anorak – keep your sense of wonder and enthusiasm*
*(cynicism will kill your joy and motivation)*

*Get some sleep when you can (you wont get much later)*

For me the moment of deep recognition came on the DVD extra when days of rehearsal, honing the message, coincided with a political move described in the newspapers that appeared to doom peace yet again, this time in Iraq. Sally and her two main actors, laid bare by fatique, sat weeping at a table, stunned and yet more determined. This is where the truth is found.

# GILLES' WIFE

*GILLES' WIFE* is a movie so French that you must read the book on which it is based in French. I don't know whether I could but I'm motivated to try, if I could afford to buy it. In the movie language is not a problem, partly because of sub-titles of course, but also because the dialogue is almost nonexistent. There are no long disquisitions on theory except in sensory visual terms.

This is a three-character drama (not counting the babies) and really the story of one person, the wife. It is her face that is stunningly eloquent. Otherwise this seamless, glowing, simple account of a woman whose sister sleeps with her husband -- throwing the man into possessive obsession and the wife into a series of wrenching internal decisions to try to wait out the affair -- has happened and been portrayed many times. Never so gorgeously.

The titles are stunning: in the steel plant where Gilles works molten metal is pouring so that against a sheet of flame and showers of sparks we see silhouettes and then one man's face marked with fatigue and soot. Quietly, he walks home across a dawning country landscape and slides into bed, then into his wife, as one continuous series. Home/bed/wife, all the same thing. His life is a rhythm of hard dangerous work and then restoration. This bonded couple nuzzles, adjusts, and pleases each other in a deeply erotic way, quite unlike Hollywood face-gnawing and thrashing. We see no one nude, nor do we see female breasts. They sit at the little kitchen table across from each other, laughing with delight at the sight of their beloved.

Into the idyll comes the wife's little sister, Victorine, growing up and ready to try out sex. When she sees a chance, she makes it clear to Gilles that she's available. He is in no need of Viagra. I get the impression that such a man is not well-explored in today's world. At least non-verbal and certainly not conscious, he is gripped by his own physiology. (He even looks like **Bob Scriver** as a young man, so you imagine the impact on me.) We never see Gilles and Victorine relate more intimately than while dancing. Gilles' passion comes out in ownership, which he attributes to deflowering her, as opposed to marrying her.

These events are context for what happens within Elisa, the wife. She struggles to understand what she should do and resolves that the only way to keep Gilles is to take his side, to help him with his obsession, even spying on his behalf. This works until Gilles loses his temper and beats Victorine, who is now ready for marriage to someone else. Everyone holds Elisa responsible for this, though she had no way of predicting it. The same people have steadfastly refused to recognize the cheating, which Victorine now blames on Elisa, too virtuous to gloat over her sister's bloodied face. In fact, she stops Gilles from inflicting worse damage.

These are the most color-coded costumes I've seen for a long time, though it's subtle. Victorine wears poppy, flame, crimson. Elisa wears Madonna blue, sometimes a strong blue, other times fading out to cool celadon. By the end of the movie they are both ashen. Gilles remains dun, khaki.

It is the Thirties in France with shooting in the distance, but the kitchen stove purrs and crackles. Material objects fascinated me, esp. a little white bowl with a red polka dot band at the top and a slender thermos for a culture where coffee is taken in very strong but small amounts. Domesticity in this stone house extends from the billowing white sheets and duvet of the bed to the terra cotta walls and tile floors of the interior to the laundry always blowing on the line to the garden moving from flowers to frost-blackened skeletons. Seasons come and go -- the story cycle takes two years so that a pregnancy (which may be partly what makes Gilles vulnerable) is completed, the baby is born (no screams or blood) and by the end he is walking. Twin girls don't age, but make it clear this is a family.

Against this is the frenzy of a carnival, a dance where things get out of hand, a cathedral so full of busy people that prayer is constantly distracted, a whole social context much bigger than home. We don't see the molten steel again except as a plume of smoke in the distance. Two important scenes were left out because they impeded the intense focus: one of Elisa drifting numbly through the busy city and the other of Gilles coming out of the factory in a street full of exhausted men.

This movie is a poem, a distillation. Many of the *imdb.com* commenters didn't catch on -- they saw it in their own modern terms, railing at Gilles for being a swine, a dummy, and considering him a narcissistic typical man as though he were today's metrosexual, casually promiscuous and psychologically defensive. The original novelist, **Madeleine Bourdouxhe**, was eight years older than **Bob Scriver** and Belgian (the background of the family on the Scriver side). *"Gilles' Wife"* was published in 1935, about the time Bob was becoming deeply involved with his first wife with much the same motivation and force as Gilles and equally disastrous results. I'm saying that I recognize this story in its own terms. It is not a feminist essay.

Many, including **Roger Ebert**, objected to the end of the movie both as an event and for what they considered "arty" camera work that up-ended the terms observed by the heroine until then: that she was patient, forgiving, understood her husband, was acting for the best, and so on -- even though she is eventually blamed by her mother, her sister, and the priest. Gilles doesn't blame her, only himself, BUT he deserts her emotionally. By the time the flames have cooled, the bed has also cooled.

It's not until a person watches the documentation of the creation of the movie that it becomes apparent how much this is a constructed art work, smooth as a shell only because it has been examined, argued, considered with huge seriousness and no restrictions except artistic ones. I was amazed to see that the "stone" house was a set. The little kitchen table that became a battleground seemed so real. But knowing that a poem is written doesn't spoil one's appreciation of it and this movie is a poem.

# M*ST*RB*T**N

Night before last I watched "*Flags of our Fathers*" and then last night "*Letters from Iwo Jima*," the **Clint Eastwood** binary about the epic WWII battle for a tiny volcanic spot in the Pacific that made our bombers able to reach Japan with our Atomic bombs. The American side centers on the raising of the flag at the top of Mount Surinam and all the misapprehension, commercialization, symbolism, and historic meaning of it, esp. the impact on Ira Hayes. The Japanese side is literally "underground" in the caves and passages an ingenious general ordered dug as defenses. But all this is another blog and maybe it's already been discussed enough.

The film needs to establish the bonding among raw troops coming from many parts of American society, a society of men who must be tough and stick together. One of the traditional means to that goal is hazing, and so the more sophisticated recruits tell the rube from Oklahoma -- who is "gee whiz" and "gung ho" to a ridiculous extent -- that he won't be able to ship out to the battle unless he has filled out his mstrbtion papers. In a barracks the practice can hardly be a secret, but this kid doesn't know the word -- it's just another big word to him. He rushes off to his commanding officer to get his mstrbtion papers in order. (I'm leaving out the vowels to baffle the web crawlers so I don't get a lot of icky spam.)

The CO was probably not amused by this corny old joke and kicked his butt, to the amusement of the so-called buddies who are really secretly preoccupied with the "c" word -- that is, courage. (Since Larkin says in his "aubade" that "courage is no good. It means not scaring others. Being brave lets no one off the grave.") So, okay, each guy is being pseudo-tough to keep from scaring others and secretly wonders whether he is brave. And mstrbtion is the shared male "secret" that is considered funny like maybe farting. It's possible to play a trick like this because knowledge about such matters is on a steep gradient between those who have no idea and those who know entirely too much and do it to the point of self-destructive pathology.

By now the researchers have established that everybody "does it." Esp. boys of a certain age when, as one scientist remarked to me, "*it's like having your you-know-what stuck into an electrical wall socket all the time.*" Girls are just better at concealing it. Researchers also know the physiology of what happens: stimulation brings blood from the rest of the body to the point of focus until it stretches all the tissues, engorging them until at some point there is a trigger that reverses the process all at once in a big rush. This feels very good. Viagra helps by supporting dilation. It was originally a heart relief drug to get the feeder arteries to open up more. And those who use it report headaches from the distention of arteries that feed the brain. (A high school student once asked me to explain what an *rg*sm was. Trying to be honest without getting fired, I told her it was like a sneeze: that is, the tension builds and builds until it discharges all at once. Forty years later she tells me my metaphor was NOT HELPFUL!)

Anyway, what's wrong with a practice that simply relieves tension, doesn't get anyone pregnant, doesn't spread disease unless one has hopelessly dirty hands or never washes other conveniences, and doesn't have to offend anyone since it's normally done privately. I suppose laundry can be a problem. And if one uses an object with too much vigor, it's possible to punch a hole in one's internal tubing that will require emergency surgery. What can be wrong with exploring one's own body and reflexes?

One problem is that human beings habituate to food and sex so easily and emotionally that a person can lose the ability to respond to anything but fetishes or paraphenalia. For a while there was a joke going around that was a variation on the "not-tonight-I-have-a-headache" -- "*Not tonight -- the vibrator is out of batteries.*" Conditioning and habituation are ways that humans get things organized and compartmented enough to think and create, or -- if you insist -- work. The movies would have you believe that without the right commercially supplied negligee, music and lighting (oh, what a fire hazard in all those banks of candles!) a physical relationship can go nowhere. There's little encouragement for simple stroking, absorbing the texture and temperature and scent of another person the way one did as a child. The entire erotic substrate of infancy is ignored, including the safety. Oh, I know. Lots of people need adrenaline, but geez! Life goes on after the excitement! If you survive.

There can be quite an anti-social bias in auto*r*ticm and a boastful tone of "I don't need no stinkin' lovers!" But flip that over, maybe through inviting voyeurism with videotape, and there is a very thin wall between auto**r*t*c*sm and torture -- doing something extreme and stimulating to oneself, where one can control and guide, can become painful and humiliating when done to someone else. Breaking taboos can hurt as much as electrical currents. And our culture already is far too guilty of linking eros with destruction, pain, power-over, and simple callousness. Some people really get off on the descriptions of torture in the news, finding it a pattern for a sick kind of intimacy, like Mailer's friend the knifer who described in "*The Belly of the Beast*" what it feels like to hold the handle of a knife with its tip against the heart of the victim.

On the other hand, curiosity about torture is parallel to curiosity about sex. Shushing and suppressing doesn't really work. Partial disclosure, especially when it doesn't allow for human empathy, can be alluring as well as lurid. Far too many kids asphyxiate themselves with a ligature to get the rush, a practice notoriously connected to "ruff s*x." They need to know MORE, not less, about what they are doing to their brains. Arousal of whatever kind can be easily reshaped by circumstances into something not intended.

Knowledge gradients -- some know too much and some know too little -- are hard to handle, esp. when matters can't be discussed. Human physiological response gradients invite too many comparisons and damning of simple differences.

Long ago I read this insight: if a grid is set up -- rigid rules about behavior and knowledge and what can be known -- that immediately creates spaces where there are no restraints because there is a total blackout. People do what cannot even be imagined by people who only know the grid. This is true of every human endeavor. In war a hidden enemy leaves us vulnerable, as it did on Iwo Jima. In business seeing those spaces is called opportunity. What do we call it in our private lives? Sometimes aren't there things it's better not to know about? Or are you one who needs to know it all? How do you find out how much knowing will hurt? Is that what happened to Ira Hayes?

www.ingramcontent.com/pod-product-compliance
Lightning Source LLC
Chambersburg PA
CBHW022116170526
45157CB00004B/1674